KEITH RICHARDS
A rock 'n' roll life

D&C
David and Charles

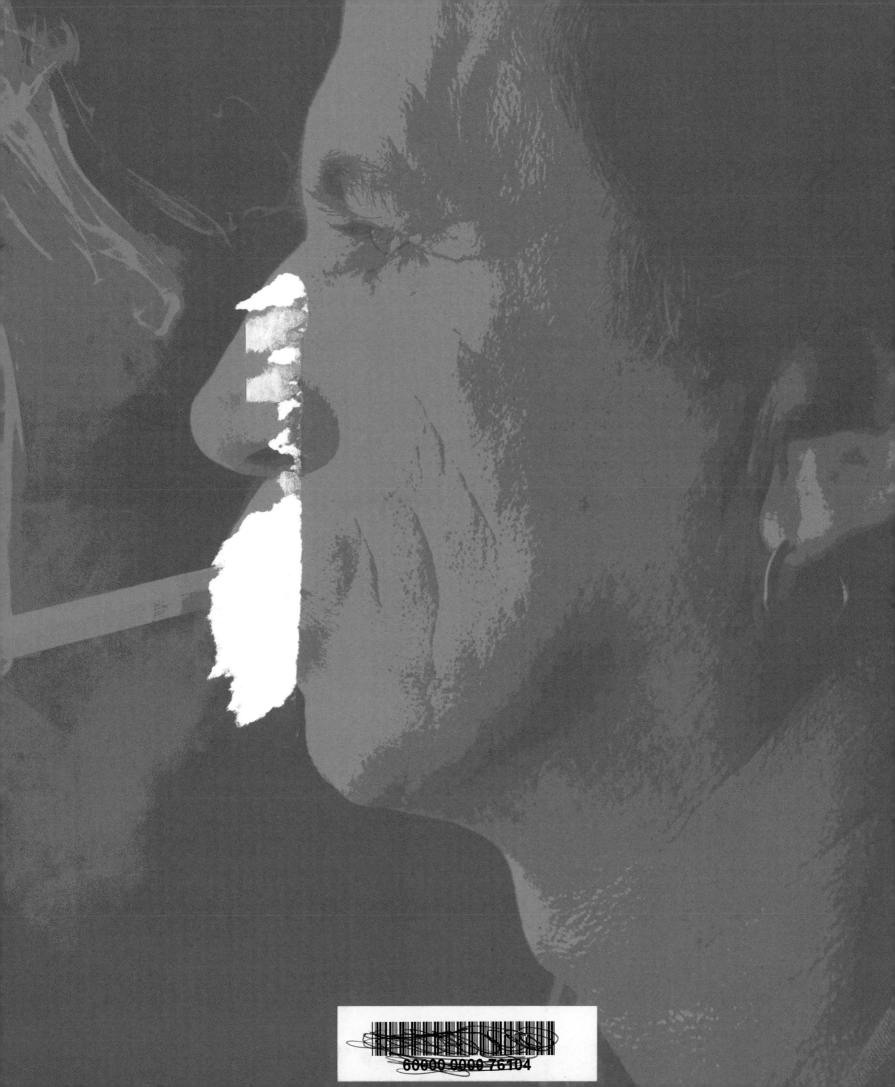

KEI

Contents

INTRODUCTION
THE IMPORTANCE OF BEING KEEF   PAGE   6

THE EARLY YEARS
DARTFORD LAD FINDS SATISFACTION   PAGE   12

ROLLING WITH THE STONES
TRIUMPHS AND TROUBLE IN PARADISE   PAGE   44

ROCK 'N' ROLL LIFER
STILL RIFFING AFTER ALL THESE YEARS   PAGE   118

TEXT BY
BILL MILKOWSKI

EDITED BY
VALERIA MANFERTO DE FABIANIS

GRAPHIC DESIGN
PAOLA PIACCO

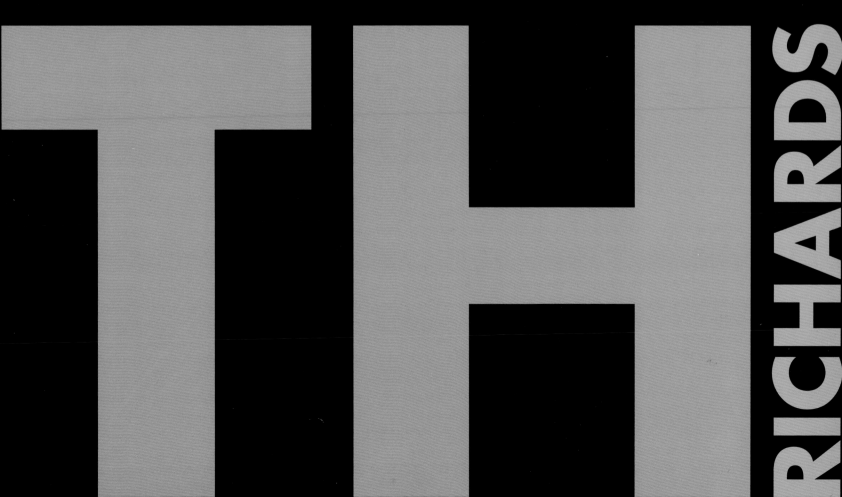

The Importance of Being Keef

He has lived a life of excess, pushing the envelope, straddling the line between order and chaos, flouting convention with an unquenchable, Dionysian spirit. And he has done so without regret. Looking at his famous craggy face now — the rough-hewn lines suggesting a relief map of his life-long journey as a rock 'n' roll road warrior — it is hard to imagine that Keith Richards was, at one time, an angel-voiced, baby-faced choirboy singing in Westminster Abbey. He claims to have slept only twice a week during the peak of his notoriety with the Rolling Stones, which means that he's probably crammed in enough activity — triumphant as well as tragic — for three lifetimes during his long and illustrious career.

A larger-than-life rock star and bona fide guitar hero (number four in *Rolling Stone* magazine's list of 100 greatest guitarists of all time), Richards' personal life has been plagued by heroin addiction and excessive recreational drug use. He's been jailed, pilloried in British tabloids, hospitalized and on the brink of death on a few occasions. And yet, he is still here. Perhaps the ultimate rock 'n' roll survivor, Richards is still rocking and rolling after all these years. And with typically sarcastic wit, he maintains that he was "kind of proud" to be number one on projected death lists for ten years in a row "I was really disappointed when I went down the charts, finally dropping down to number nine," he wrote in his best-selling memoir, 'Life.'

As he once told *NME* magazine, "I've no pretensions about immortality."

My own personal memories of Keith go back to my 1960s childhood. Growing up in Milwaukee — just down the road from Chicago — I was aware of all the same blues heroes that Richards worshipped as a lad growing up in Dartford, England: Muddy Waters, Howlin' Wolf, Jimmy Reed, Little Walter and others. Through my older guitar-playing brother, Tom, I was hipped to Fats Domino, Jerry Lee Lewis, the Coasters, Gary U.S. Bonds along with the music of funky New Orleans piano masters Professor Longhair and Eddie Bo. So I was primed for the Rolling Stones when they came along with *England's Newest Hit Makers*, *12X5* and the *Rolling Stones, Now!* at the peak of the British Invasion. Seeing them playing "Satisfaction," "She Said Yeah" and "Get Off of My Cloud" on the NBC musical variety TV show *Hullabaloo* on 15 November 1965 was a revelation — Brian Jones and Keith Richards with matching Gibson Firebird guitars and black-sounding Mick Jagger with impossibly fat lips and wiry moves. As for my brother, Tom, I'll let him weigh in here about the effect that the Rolling Stones, and Keith Richards in particular, had on him back then:

"I heard the Beatles first, of course. Then I had a girlfriend who was into the Stones. So to impress this chick, I made it a point to check out all the Stones recordings I could find. This was in 1965, but be-

FORE "TH LAST TIME" AND "SATISFACTION" CAME OUT. THEIR TOP SELLING SONGS AT THAT TIME WERE "TELL ME," "HEART OF STONE" AND "LITTLE RED ROOSTER," BUT MY EARLY FAVORITE WAS "NOT FADE AWAY." THEY TOOK THIS BUDDY HOLLY POP SONG AND TURNED IT INTO A WICKED BO DIDDLEY BEAT WITH HARMONICA, ACOUSTIC AND ELECTRIC GUITARS, WHICH WAS MUCH MORE EXCITING TO ME THAN THE BEATLES' COVER SONGS THAT SOUNDED LILY WHITE BY COMPARISON. THEY HAD THE PRIMAL BEAT AND AUTHENTIC BLACK SOUND DOWN PAT. I WILL ARGUE THAT IT WAS FAR MORE EMOTIONALLY POWERFUL THAN THE BEATLES."

IN TERMS OF SHEER GUITAR PLAYING, BROTHER TOM WAS FAR MORE DRAWN TO KEITH RICHARDS THAN GEORGE HARRISON. AS HE EXPLAINS, "GEORGE WAS INFLUENCED MORE BY CARL PERKINS AND BUDDY HOLLY AND OTHER WHITE PLAYERS. WHEN I STARTED DIGGING THE STONES' LPS, I REMEMBER SKIPPING THE NEEDLE AHEAD TO KEITH'S GUITAR SOLOS FOR EACH CUT ON THE ALBUM. HE WAS NEVER SUPER-FLASHY, BUT HE HAD COOL BLACK-INFLUENCED LICKS THAT I THOUGHT I COULD LEARN. AND THE SOUND HE GOT WAS SO PERFECT FOR EVERY SONG. IT WAS OBVIOUS THAT THE STONES LIVED AND BREATHED THIS R&B MUSIC AND SPENT A LOT OF TIME GETTING THE STUDIO SOUND JUST RIGHT. THEIR RHYTHMS WERE SO MUCH COOLER THAN WHAT THE BEATLES WERE DOING AND I BET KEITH WAS THE MAIN GUY RESPONSIBLE FOR THEIR SOUND RIGHT FROM THE BEGINNING. HE WAS THE ANTI-GEORGE HARRISON, IN MY VIEW."

WHEN THE STONES FINALLY ROLLED INTO TOWN, AND TOM GOT TO SEE THEM IN CONCERT AT THE MILWAUKEE ARENA, HE WAS FURTHER TAKEN BY THEIR PROTO-PUNK STANCE. "I ADMIRED THEIR DEFIANT ATTITUDE. SHIT, THESE WERE GUYS THAT SURELY PISSED WHEREVER THEY WANTED TO. PARENTS AND CHICKS IN SCHOOL PRETTY MUCH LIKED AND ACCEPTED THE ASS-KISSING, PRETTY-BOY BEATLES, BUT THE STONES WERE FOR US RENEGADES."

AS A RIFFMEISTER OF THE HIGHEST ORDER, KEITH'S DIRECT, INCISIVE AND INVENTIVE GUITAR LICKS DEFINED SUCH ICONIC TUNES AS "SATISFACTION," "START ME UP," "BROWN SUGAR," "JUMPIN' JACK FLASH" AND "HONKY TONK WOMEN." A DISCIPLE OF SUCH GREAT GUITARISTS AND PIONEERING ROCKERS AS SCOTTY MOORE AND CHUCK BERRY AND BLUESMEN LIKE MUDDY WATERS AND JIMMY REED, RICHARDS (NICKNAMED 'KEEF' AS A LAD) FORGED A PERSONAL VOCABULARY ON THE INSTRUMENT THAT HAS INFLUENCED GENERATIONS OF ASPIRING ROCKERS.

NILS LOFGREN, GUITARIST IN BRUCE SPRINGSTEEN'S E-STREET BAND, REMEMBERS BEING TURNED ON IN JUNIOR HIGH SCHOOL BY HEARING "SATISFACTION" AND LATER STANDING IN AWE OF THE DARK AND SINISTER MOOD THAT KEITH CONJURED UP IN THE OPENING TO "GIMME SHELTER." AS HE TOLD *ROLLING STONE* MAGAZINE: "KEITH WROTE TWO-AND THREE-NOTE THEMES THAT WERE MORE POWERFUL THAN ANY GREAT SOLO. I WENT TO SEE KEITH WITH THE X-PENSIVE WINOS. IN THE DRESSING ROOM, KEITH STARTED PRACTICING A CHUCK BERRY RIFF. I'D NEVER IN MY LIFE HEARD IT SOUND LIKE THAT. I LOVE CHUCK BERRY. BUT THIS WAS BETTER. NOT TECHNICALLY – THERE WAS AN EMOTIONAL CONTENT THAT SPOKE TO ME. WHAT CHUCK IS TO KEITH, KEITH IS TO ME."

AS RICHARDS HIMSELF SAID OF THAT ELUSIVE QUALITY THAT TOUCHED LOFGREN AND GENERATIONS OF GUITAR PLAYERS WHO FOLLOWED: "CHUCK GOT IT FROM T-BONE WALKER, AND I GOT IT FROM CHUCK, MUDDY WATERS, ELMORE JAMES AND B.B. KING. WE'RE ALL PART OF THIS FAMILY THAT GOES BACK THOUSANDS OF YEARS. REALLY, WE'RE ALL PASSING IT ON."

APART FROM HIS GUITAR-PLAYING PROWESS, RICHARDS HAS ALSO SECURED A SPOT IN THE SONGWRITERS HALL OF FAME AS ONE-HALF OF THE INDELIBLE JAGGER-RICHARDS TEAM WITH HIS LIFELONG FRIEND/FOE AND SONGWRITING PARTNER, MICK JAGGER. THEIRS HAS BEEN AN ALTERNATELY KINDRED AND CONFOUNDING PARTNERSHIP FOR OVER 50 YEARS AND CONTINUES TO THIS DAY, MARKED BY INSPIRED CREATIVITY AND PETTY JEALOUSIES.

I WAS LUCKY ENOUGH TO HAVE INTERVIEWED RICHARDS IN 1988 WHEN HE WAS PROMOTING HIS SOLO DEBUT ALBUM *TALK IS CHEAP*. HE WAS 44 YEARS OLD AT THE TIME BUT LOOKED 20 YEARS OLDER. HE CHAIN-SMOKED CIGARETTES AND DRANK JACK DANIELS THROUGHOUT THE COURSE OF THE HOUR-LONG INTERVIEW AND WAS GENUINELY VERY ENGAGING AND FORTHCOMING IN ALL OF HIS ANSWERS TO MY VARIOUS QUESTIONS. HE LISTENED INTENTLY AND RESPONDED IN THE MOMENT, GIVING ME THE IMPRESSION THAT WE WERE TRULY HAVING A CONVERSATION RATHER THAN HIM JUST RECITING THE SAME ROTE ANSWERS THAT HE MAY HAVE GIVEN COUNTLESS TIMES BEFORE TO OTHER EAGER INTERVIEWERS. AT THE END, I MENTIONED THAT HIS PAL, BLUES GUITARIST ROBERT CRAY, WAS PERFORMING IN TOWN THAT NIGHT AND ASKED IF HE WAS PLANNING TO SWING BY HIS GIG AND MAYBE SIT IN. KEITH LAUGHED AND SAID IN HIS GRAVELLY PIRATE VOICE, "NO, MATE. I'VE GOT BABY-SITTING DUTY TONIGHT," REFERRING TO HIS DAUGHTERS ALEXANDRA AND THEODORA, WHO WERE TWO AND THREE YEARS OLD, RESPECTIVELY, AT THE TIME.

I GOT THE SENSE FROM OUR CHAT THAT KEITH WAS A REAL DOWN TO EARTH GUY BUT WONDERED IN THAT MOMENT IF THE ROLLING STONES WOULD INDEED SURVIVE THE SEPARATE SOLO CAREERS OF RICHARDS AND JAGGER. AS KEITH HAD TOLD ME, "MICK AND I ARE STILL SORT OF TESTING EACH OTHER AT THIS POINT. BUT I LOVE THE GUY. I LOVE TO WORK WITH HIM. THERE ARE CERTAIN THINGS ABOUT WHAT HE'S DONE THAT PISS ME OFF, BUT NOTHING MORE THAN WHAT GOES DOWN WITH ANY FRIENDS, REALLY. IF YOU CAN'T LEAN ON YOUR MATE THEN YOU'RE NOT REALLY HIS FRIEND, RIGHT? THEN YOU'RE AN ACQUAINTANCE, NOT A FRIEND. MICK AND I GO A LITTLE BIT BEYOND JUST BEING ABLE TO INSULT EACH OTHER. IT'S NOT JUST TWO RICH SUPERSTARS INDULGING IN A POWER STRUGGLE. IT'S ABOUT US TRYING TO FIND EACH OTHER AT THIS POINT. AND I THINK AT THIS POINT, MICK IS PROBABLY REALIZING THAT HE REALLY NEEDS THE ROLLING STONES MORE THAN ACTUALLY THE ROLLING STONES NEED MICK."

NEARLY 25 YEARS AFTER MY INITIAL ENCOUNTER WITH KEITH, WE'RE BOTH OLDER AND WISER. AND WHILE THE CLASS-CONSCIOUS SIR MICK JAGGER (HE WAS KNIGHTED ON 12 DECEMBER 2003) MAY PREFER THE COMPANY OF CELEBRITIES, ROYALTY AND THE POWER ELITE, I'M CONVINCED THAT KEITH IS AN UNPRETENTIOUS GUY WHO IS HAPPY TO HANG WITH HIS MATES, JUST JAMMING IN THE L-SHAPED BASEMENT OF HIS CONNECTICUT HOME, WHERE HE LIVES WITH HIS WIFE OF NEARLY 30 YEARS, ONE-TIME SUPER MODEL PATTI HANSEN.

"I'M THE SAME AS EVERYONE," HE ONCE TOLD *NME*, "JUST KIND OF LUCKY."

KEITH'S LUCK HAS NOT YET RUN OUT. HE MAY OUTLIVE US ALL. AND NO DOUBT GO OUT ROCKIN.'

2 Flashing his prized skull ring.

3 At the Union Club on London's Greek Street, 19 September 1995.

4 On tour with The New Barbarians, a side project in 1979 that featured Rolling Stones bandmate Ronnie Wood, Return To Forever bassist Stan-ley Clarke and The Meters' drummer Zigaboo Modeliste.

7 Dazed and dejected outside his gutted Redlands home after a fire in August 1973.

10-11 Striking a rebellious pose in 1981.

The Early Years

DARTFORD LAD FINDS SATISFACTION

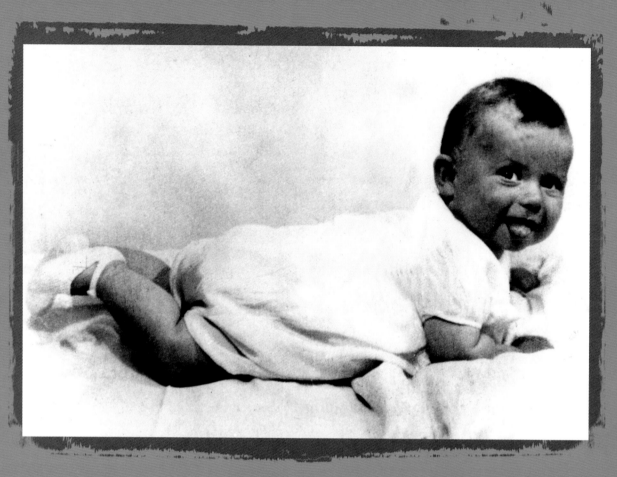

KEITHRICHARDS

Keith had an undistinguished start. Born to Bert and Doris Richards on 18 December 1943, he grew up in post-war England on the Dartford marshes, along the River Thames in East London. As an only child, he was given a relatively comfortable suburban life by his working class parents and attended Wentworth Primary School, with another boy who would figure prominently in Keith's future. His name was Mick Jagger. He lived just a few doors from Keith in Dartford, but it wasn't until a few years later that the two boys would explore their mutual love of African-American blues and R&B music together by finally forming an amateur band.

It was Keith's grandfather Gus (his mother's father) who introduced him to the guitar, letting him pick out melodies on his classical Spanish guitar at the age of nine and, eventually, showing Keith his first licks and chords. Harmonizing with his aunt Joanna to Everly Brothers songs around the house was also part of Keith's musical upbringing. But it was hearing the likes of Elvis Presley, Little Richard, Chuck Berry, Buddy Holly, Jerry Lee Lewis, Fats Domino and Eddie Cochran on Radio Luxembourg that captured his imagination and launched him on a path that he's been pursuing to this day. From his teens, rock 'n' roll became an addiction for Keith as powerful as the narcotics he indulged in during his most decadent adult years.

His mum bought him his first guitar, in 1959. A year later, he happened to see his boyhood hero Chuck Berry in *Jazz on a Summer's Day,* Bert Stern's documentary about the 1958 Newport Jazz Festival. In a November 2011 issue of *Rolling Stone* magazine, Richards described the impact that Berry had on him: "When I saw Chuck Berry in *Jazz on a Summer's Day* as a teenager, what struck me was how he was playing against the grain with a bunch of jazz guys. They were brilliant – guys like Jo Jones on drums and Jack Teagarden on trombone – but they had that jazz attitude cats put on sometimes: 'Ooh...this rock 'n' roll...' But Chuck took them all by storm and played against their animosity. To me, that's blues. That's the attitude and the guts it takes. That's what I wanted to be, except I was white."

"I listened to every lick he played and picked it up. Chuck was playing a slightly heated-up version of Chicago blues, that guitar boogie – which all the cats were playing – but he took it up to another level. Chuck had the swing. There's rock, but it's the roll that counts. And Chuck had an incredible band on those early records: Willie Dixon on bass, Johnnie Johnson on piano, Ebby Hardy or Freddy Below on drums. They understood what he was about and just swung with it. It don't get any better than that."

By that time, Keith and Mick Jagger had long since fallen out of touch. Several years had gone by since their last encounter at Wentworth Primary School. Richards was now attending Sidcup Art College, having been expelled from Dartford Tech for truancy, and Jagger was attending the London School of Economics. But they would have a fateful reunion at Dartford railway station on the morning of 17 December 1961. Keith was standing on the platform that day, waiting for a train and holding one of Chuck Berry's records. He was spotted by Mick, who approached Richards to inquire about his musical tastes. It turned out that Jagger too was a Chuck Berry fanatic and part of a loose aggregation of fellow music lovers who met every Saturday morning at a juke joint in Dartford to listen to American rock 'n' roll and R&B records. Mick invited Keith to attend one of their weekend record-listening parties and from that moment their friendship blossomed.

The two kindred souls began record-hunting together, searching for any Chuck Berry, Buddy Holly, Eddie Cochran, Jimmy Reed, B.B. King, Little Milton and Muddy Waters albums they could find at local shops. By that time, Jagger was also getting a healthy supply of blues and R&B records delivered to him, via mail order, from Chess Records in Chicago. And his massive collection was the envy of every blues hound and record collector in town, including Richards.

Occasionally, Mick and Keith would travel together, by car, to Manchester to see blues revues featuring such legends as John Lee Hooker, Memphis Slim, Junior Wells, Buddy Guy and Hubert Sumlin. It seemed they instinctively gravitated to the real deal when it came to the blues. They had identical tastes in terms of which artists were faking it and which ones were the real deal. And they emulated that sense of authenticity in their own early music-making endeavours.

During the summer of 1961, while on a family trip to Devon, a 17-year-old Keith and an 18-year-old Mick played together casually in a pub to a favorable response. By the end of the year, they joined with Keith's fellow Sidcup schoolmate Dick Taylor on bass, Bob Beckwith on guitar and Allen Etherington on drums as Little Boy Blue and the Blue Boys, with frontman Jagger cast as Little Boy Blue. Some of the first tunes they learned included Buddy Holly's "That'll Be The Day" and "Not Fade Away," Chuck Berry's "Reel-in' and Rockin,'" Jimmy Reed's "Bright Lights, Big City" and Muddy Waters' "I Just Want To Make Love To You."

They played their first gigs as Little Boy Blue and the Blue Boys at the Ealing Jazz Club in London. Alexis Korner, father of the London blues scene, also played there every week with his Blues Incorporated, which included a young Charlie Watts on drums and Ian Stewart on piano. It's also where Mick and Keith met Brian Jones (full name Lewis Brian Hopkins Jones), who was playing slide guitar at the time and billing himself as Elmo Lewis (in tribute to the great Delta blues slide guitarist Elmore James). Though Richards acknowledged Jones' talent and depth of musical knowledge (indeed, Brian became a kind of mentor figure for Keith, turning him onto Delta blues icons like Robert Johnson and Son House), he also saw a cruel, manipulative, cold-blooded streak in the short, blond-haired guitarist from Cheltenham; a dark, foreboding characteristic that would later play out in tragic terms.

By the Spring of 1962, Brian Jones and Ian Stewart had decided to form an R&B band. They recruited Jagger and Richards, Dick Taylor on bass and future Kinks drummer Mick Avory. Initially, they called themselves The Rollin' Stones, after a favorite Muddy Waters song, "Rollin' Stone." Their first gig as The Rolling Stones (with Tony Chapman on drums) was on 12 July 1962 at the Marquee in London. Their set included covers of Jimmy Reed's "Bright Lights, Big City" and "Big Boss Man," Chuck Berry's "Back in the USA," Willie Dixon's "Baby What's Wong?," Elmore James' "Happy Home" and "Dust My Broom," Billy Boy Arnold's "I Ain't Got You" and a rockin' version the 1946 Amos Milburn boogie-woogie hit "Down the Road a Piece."

Over the course of the next few months they honed their raw renditions of tunes by Chuck Berry, Bo Diddley and Buddy Holly along with the tough Chicago blues sound of Jimmy Reed and Muddy Waters. Over time, Keith would develop an intricate, interlocking chemistry with his six-string partner Jones, emulating such potent two-guitar teams as Muddy Waters and Jimmy Rogers, Howlin' Wolf and Hubert Sumlin, or the Myers brothers (Louis and David), who played behind harmonica star Little Walter. In eagerly promoting the music of Chicago blues artists in their own gigs, the Rolling Stones turned a generation of young Brits on to these quintessentially American sounds.

In the late summer of 1962, Mick, Keith and Brian moved into a dingy flat together in Fulham. Taking low-paying gigs at school dances (often playing just for beers), they barely pulled together enough money to pay the rent each month and often resorted to shoplifting groceries to fend off hunger. By September they had landed a regular weekly gig at the Ealing Jazz Club and in January 1963 they secured a Sunday afternoon residency at the Crawdaddy Club, a popular underground scene in the Richmond Station Hotel run by audacious entrepreneur Giorgio Gomelsky, who began an informal relationship as their manager.

By late January 1963, bassist Bill Wyman had joined the band. His powerful Vox amp gave The Rolling Stones a low-end punch that they hadn't previously had. They also got an upgrade after acquiring the services of in-demand drummer Charlie Watts, whom they had been trying to recruit for several months. Watts had sat in with the band in late 1962 but was unwilling to give up his higher-paying gig with Blues Incorporated (which also included Jack Bruce on upright bass, Alexis Korner on guitar, Dick Heckstall-Smith on saxophone, Keith Scott on piano, Cyril Davies on harmonica and Long John Baldry on vocals). When Brian, Mick, Keith and the crew were finally able to meet Watts' asking price, he officially joined the Rolling Stones on 2 February 1963 and, instantly, his solid backbeat lifted the band to a new level (his place in Blues Incorporated would be filled by future Cream drummer Ginger Baker).

Richards has frequently commented in interviews about the attributes that Charlie Watts brought to the band, referring to his great feel and ability to stretch out the beat as 'the secret of the Rolling Stones sound.' As he put it in a video clip in the Ask Keith section of his website (www.keithrichards.com): Without a great drummer it's such hard work to just keep the thing going. But great drummers, they give you the freedom to do what you

AN EARLY "ANTI-BEATLES" PROMOTIONAL SLOGAN READ: "WOULD YOU LET YOUR DAUGHTER MARRY A ROLLING STONE?"

want to do. You don't feel tied down, and that's really what it is all about. And Charlie is one of the greatest drummers the damn world is ever going to see ... so beautifully spontaneous with a tremendous amount of personality and subtlety in his playing; a constant source of enjoyment. He's got the moves. Charlie Watts has always been the bed that I lie on musically."

Bassist Bill Wyman explains the secret of the Rolling Stones' unique time feel this way: "Simple. Charlie drags, Keith rushes, and I play right down the middle." That delightful rhythmic tug-of-war would come to define their chemistry for decades.

It was at their regular gig, at the cramped Crawdaddy Club, that this newest edition of The Rolling Stones was spotted by Andrew Loog Oldham, a former publicist for the Beatles. He soon replaced Gomelsky as the band's official manager, in April 1963, and quickly negotiated a deal for them with Decca Records, promoting them as "The Anti-Beatles" by playing on their rougher bad-boy image in contrast to the cutesy, uniform-wearing, mop-topped Fab Four. One of Oldham's early promotional campaigns for the band included the provocative slogan: "Would you let your daughter marry a Rolling Stone?"

Their first Decca single, a cover of Chuck Berry's "Come On," was released on 7 June 1963. The B-side was Willie Dixon's "I Want to Be Loved," which featured Jones on harmonica. On 23 August, they lip-synched to "Come On" on the popular BBC TV show, *Ready, Steady, Go!* In September the Rolling Stones set out on a five-week tour of the UK (from 23 September to 3 November), opening for the Everly Brothers, Bo Diddley and Little Richard. As Richards recalls, "That was an incredible line-up. We felt like we were in Disneyland, or the best theme park we could imagine."

On 7 October, the Stones recorded their second single, a cover of the Lennon-McCartney tune "I Wanna Be Your Man." The flip side was the Jagger-Richards-Jones original, "Stoned." It was released on 1 November to acclaim in the UK. On their second UK tour, from 7 February to 3 March of 1964, the Stones toured with the popular American girl group The Ronettes. Keith would have a brief romance with the group's lead singer, Ronnie Bennett, who was involved at the time with producer Phil Spector. As Keith recalls, "We were 20 years old and we just fell in love. But basically, it was just hormones."

It was the Stones' third Decca single, a cover of Buddy Holly's "Not Fade Away," B-side of the original "Little By Little," that registered their first real chart success, reaching number three by late February 1964. Their self-titled debut album for Decca, recorded in England on 16 April 1964, included energised covers of Willie

12 Decked out in herringbone jacket, with acoustic guitar.

14 As a baby, in Dartford, England, 1944.

18 The Rolling Stones in Chelsea, London, 1963. From left to right: Keith Richards, Bill Wyman, Mick Jagger, Brian Jones, Charlie Watts.

Dixon's "I Just Want To Make Love To You," Bobby Troup's "Route 66," Jimmy Reed's "Honest I Do," Chuck Berry's "Carol," Slim Harpo's "I'm a King Bee" and Rufus Thomas' "Walking the Dog" along with the first Jagger-Richards original, "Tell Me (You're Coming Back Again)." The album was released in the United States on London Records as *England's Newest Hit Makers* on 30 May 1964.

During the Stones' first US tour, in June of 1964, they visited Chicago's Chess Studios, where they met their hero Muddy Waters and also recorded versions of Jerry Ragovoy's "Time Is On My Side" (which had been a regional hit for New Orleans' Queen of Soul Irma Thomas) and Bobby Womack's "It's All Over Now," which subsequently became the band's first number one UK hit. They also made appearances on several popular American TV shows during that tour, including *The Hollywood Palace*, hosted that evening by a sardonic Dean Martin, who mocked the boys' long hair on-air. But the Stones didn't let his insulting comments get in the way of energised performances of "Not Fade Away" and "I Just Want To Make Love To You." On the popular Cleveland-based *The Mike Douglas Show*, they performed versions of Chuck Berry's "Carol," "Not Fade Away," "Tell Me" and "I Just Want To Make Love To You" while also submitting to the host's demeaning questions in an interview session.

Back in England, the Stones released another single on 26 June, "It's All Over Now" B-side of the Jagger-Richards original "Good Times, Bad Times," which they performed that same day on *Ready, Steady, Go!* In November they cut "Heart of Stone," which included accompanying work by session guitarists John McLaughlin and Jimmy Page. They toured the UK again from 5 September to 11 October. Their second London album, *12X5*, was released on 17 October and was followed by a second US tour (24 October to 15 November), which included their first appearance (25 October) on *The Ed Sullivan Show*. Their rocking renditions of Chuck Berry's "Around and Around" and "Time Is On My Side" left the American audience breathless. Then on 29 October at the Santa Monica Civic Center, the Rolling Stones appeared on the *Teen Age Music International (TAMI) Awards Show* along with the likes of Smokey Robinson and the Miracles, The Supremes, Marvin Gaye and James Brown. Their versions of "Around and Around," "Time Is On My Side," "It's All Over Now" and "I'm Alright" thrilled fans, although Jagger's attempts to out-do the Godfather of Soul fell flat. After Brown unleashed his one-legged slides across stage, razor-sharp dance moves, splits and 'The Camel Walk' on national TV during an explosive rendition of "Night Train," Mick's on stage moves seemed meager by comparison.

Near the end of that second US tour in 1964, the Stones recorded material, at the RCA Studios in Hollywood and Chess Studios in Chicago, that would subsequently appear on their third London album *Rolling Stones, Now!* (released in the US on 13 February 1965). It included covers of Solomon Burke's "Everybody Needs Somebody to Love," Jerry Leiber's "Down Home Girl," Allen Toussaint's "Pain in My Heart," Bo Diddley's "Mona (I Need You Baby)," Chuck Berry's "You Can't Catch Me" and the Jagger-Richards originals, "Heart of Stone" and "What a Shame."

The rootsy *Rolling Stones, Now!* also included appropriately greasy interpretations of the 1946 Amos Milburn boogie woogie hit "Down the Road a Piece" and Barbara Lynn's driving R&B number "Oh Baby (We Got a Good Thing Goin' On)." The Stones followed with a string of hit singles in the UK. Their cover of Willie Dixon's "Little Red Rooster" (B-side of the Jagger-Richards original "Off The Hook") reached number one in the UK on 5 December 1964. The riff-oriented Jagger-Richards original "The Last Time" (B-side the darkly menacing "Play With Fire") reached number one in the UK in March 1965. And the fuzz tone-fuelled "(I Can't Get No) Satisfaction" reached number one in the UK in August 1965, although it had already been released in the US in June (its UK release was delayed because its lyrics were initially deemed too sexually suggestive).

"Satisfaction," which appeared on the American release of *Out of Our Heads*, was the Stones' first number one hit single in the US (B-side in the US was "The Under Assistant West Coast Promotion Man" while in the UK the B-side was "The Spider and the Fly"). That controversial tune, with pointed lyrics referring to sexual frustration and rampant commercialism that they had seen in America, was sung by Jagger with an angry sneer and rare authority, backed by a catchy three-note guitar riff from Keith. Its overwhelming popularity quickly catapulted the Stones to international fame.

In retrospect, Richards feels that the impact of "Satisfaction" at that moment may have had something to do with shifting social mores in America, that the lyrics and mood of the song tapped into youth's growing disenchantment with the 'grown-up world.' Or it could've just been that infectious three-note riff of Keith's (one of the rare times in his recording career that he ever used a fuzz tone on his guitar).

Earlier in 1965, the Stones had continued their assault on America with a third US tour along with a second appearance on *The Ed Sullivan Show* (that 2 May show included performances of their current hit "The Last Time" along with renditions of "Little Red Rooster," "Everybody Needs Somebody to Love" and "2120 South Michigan Avenue," an instrumental from *12X5* which was also the address of Chess Records, where they recorded the tune). Three weeks later (on 20 May), they made an appearance on *Shindig!*, the West Coast ABC counterpart to NBC's New York-based *Hullabaloo*. Not only did the Stones perform versions of "Little Red Rooster," "Play With Fire," "The Last Time" and "Satisfaction" but they also, literally, sat at the feet of their hero, blues legend Howlin' Wolf, staring adoringly as he performed "How Many More Years" with Billy Preston on piano and James Burton on guitar.

The Stones juggernaut rolled through the US again in November 1965, concluding their fourth US tour with highly-rated TV appearances on *Shindig!*, where they turned in spirited covers of Sam Cooke's "Good Times" and Don Covay's "Mercy Mercy" and a week later on *Hullabaloo*, where they performed "She Said Yeah" and "Get Off Of My Cloud," their follow-up single to the mega-hit "Satisfaction."

With the success of "Satisfaction" and "Get Off Of My Cloud" behind them, the Rolling Stones rode The British Invasion (which included The Beatles, The Animals, The Kinks and The Dave Clark Five) like a global tidal wave. And yet, bigger things were on the horizon for Keith and the boys.

22-23 Early publicity shot of The Rolling Stones, in London, 1963. From left to right: Bill Wyman, Mick Jagger, a slightly tipsy Keith Richards, Charlie Watts, Brian Jones.

24 and 25 A joung Keith Richards (left), circa 1963. Backstage at The Great Pop Prom at the Royal Albert Hall, where The Rolling Stones performed during the afternoon of 15 September 1963 (right).

26 With Brian Jones, trading licks backstage, December 1963

27 With Brian Jones making faces backstage at The Mod Ball, circa 1963

28 The Rolling Stones performing outside at Longleat House, home of the Marquis of Bath, 2 August 1964.

29 The Rolling Stones outside the Hotel Astor on Central Park West, New York during their first visit to America, 2 June 1964.

KEITHRICHARDS

30-31 Mayhem at The Glad Rag Ball held at the Empire Pool, Wembley, London, 20 November 1964.

31 Signing autographs outside the Ed Sullivan Theater on Broadway, 2 June 1964.

32-33 The Rolling Stones experiencing their first New York diner, 2 June 1964.

KEITHRICHARDS

34-35 In the early stages of his life-long career as a smoker.

35 Relaxing on tour in Hamburg, circa 1964.

36 Being fitted for a suit at Beau Gentry on North Vine Street in Hollywood, 4 June 1964.

37 Posing in a new suit at Beau Gentry on North Vine Street in Hollywood, 4 June 1964.

38 21 years old, circa 1965.

39 Playing a Vox Mark XII 12-string electric guitar on the set of TV's "Ready Steady Go!" in London, 26 June 1965.

40 With Mick Jagger on TV's "The Clay Cole Show" in New York, 2 May 1965.

42-43 In repose with acoustic guitar, circa 1964-1965.

STEEPED IN RAUCOUS BLUES AND R&B, **THE JAGGER-RICHARDS SONGWRITING TEAM** OCCASIONALLY CAME UP WITH A TENDER GEM LIKE "AS TEARS GO BY."

Rolling with
the Stones

TRIUMPHS AND TROUBLE IN PARADISE

The Rolling Stones' fifth album, *December's Children (And Everybody's)*, rushed out in December 1965, followed the same formula of half Jagger-Richards originals and half well-chosen covers. Their originals included the memorable "Get Off Of My Cloud," which had already been a number one hit single in October 1965, "Blue Turns to Grey," "The Singer Not The Song" and "I'm Free" (which had been B-side to "Get Off Of My Cloud"). They also turned in faithful covers of Chuck Berry's "Talkin' About You," Arthur Alexander's "You Better Move On," Muddy Waters' "Look What You've Done" and Bobby Troup's "Route 66" along with a revved-up rendition of country star Hank Snow's "I'm Movin' On." The album also included a version of "As Tears Go By," the tune that Jagger, Richards and Oldham had written in 1964 for Marianne Faithfull, who would later have a highly publicized romance with Jagger. The Stones' poignant rendition, with lush string arrangements by Mike Leander, was seen by critics as an answer to Paul McCartney's "Yesterday," though Jagger and Richards had actually written the song with manager-producer Oldham a full year earlier. A single of "As Tears Go By" was released in the US on 18 December 1965 (B-side was "Gotta Get Away"). It was released in the UK (on 4 February 1966) as B-side to the Stones next number one single, "19th Nervous Breakdown."

With the release of the adventurous *Aftermath*, their sixth album and their first of all-original material, the Stones made a significant leap forward. Producer Andrew Loog Oldham had been encouraging them to get away from covers of material by R&B and blues artists from America and focus more on song-writing. And the team of Jagger-Richards delivered on this album with strong tunes like "Doncha

Bother Me" and "It's Not Easy," which were still imbued with the rootsy vibe that had permeated their early covers, along with edgier numbers like the organ-fuelled "Stupid Girl" and the hard-hitting "Flight 505," both of which carried a proto-punk sneer that would soon become the Stones' calling card.

Elsewhere on *Aftermath*, released in April in the UK and June in the US, the Stones pushed the boundaries with more experimental fare like the minor key, Indian raga flavoured "Paint it Black" (their sixth number one single in the UK, featuring Jones on sitar), the delicate Elizabethan ballad "Lady Jane" which utilized dulcimer and harpsichord, the meditative "I Am Waiting," the jazzy "Under My Thumb" (with Jones on marimba) and the 11-minute blues jam "Goin' Home," punctuated by Jagger's breathy, histrionic improv vocals over a sinister, coolly-understated but percolating groove.

At the end of 1966, the Stones released a poorly recorded live album, *Got Live If You Want It*, which was further marred by the constant screaming of teenage girls in the audience. Released as part of a contractual obligation to US distributor London Records, it was culled from material recorded on tour in the UK in March of 1965. Given its inferior quality, it was quickly dismissed by critics and practically dis-owned by the band members, though fans enjoyed hearing concert versions of the Stones' new singles "Have You Seen Your Mother, Baby, Standing in the Shadow?" and "Get Off Of My Cloud" along with remakes of "(I Can't Get No) Satisfaction," "The Last Time," the Bo Diddley influenced "19th Nervous Breakdown" (which had been released as a single earlier that year with "Sad Day" as the B-side) and a smouldering cover of Otis Redding's "I've Been Loving You Too Long."

By the end of 1966, the Stones were exhausted from almost constant roadwork over the previous four years. The band's sudden success had also begun to have adverse effects on Brian Jones, whose drug intake only fueled his out-of-control ego and neurotic need for adulation. "I never saw a guy so much affected by fame," said Keith, who described Jones as a perpetual pain in the neck on the road, a dead weight on their gruelling tour of one-nighters.

The Rolling Stones got back on track with two eclectic but controversial studio albums released back-to-back in 1967 – *Between the Buttons* and *Flowers*, both admired only by the most ardent devo-tees. *Between the Buttons* (released on 20 January in the UK and 11 February in the US) includes tunes like "Let's Spend the Night Together," "Yesterday's Papers," the brooding "Ruby Tuesday" (with Jones playing recorder) and the romantic "She Smiled Sweetly," all of which show a more refined sense of song and lyric writing from the Jagger-Richards team. Meanwhile, "Connection" and "Miss Amanda Jones" retained the raw, rocking firepower of their rootsy, youthful beginnings. The album's closer, "Something Happened To Me Yesterday," reportedly about an LSD trip, had Richards alternating on lead vocals with Mick.

On 15 January 1967, The Rolling Stones had made their fifth appearance on *The Ed Sullivan Show*. Mick Jagger was forced to change the words of "Let's Spend The Night Together" to "Let's spend some time together" to appease censors. Sullivan, the powerful host of the influential TV variety show, had told Jagger, "Either the song goes or you go." Jagger agreed to amend the lyrics, though he could be seen rolling his eyes on camera while singing the passage in question, which infuriated Sullivan and resulted in their being banned from his show in the future.

Flowers, an American compilation released in June, during the so-called 'Summer of Love,' was cobbled together from previously-released singles or tunes left out of the American versions of *Aftermath* and *Between the Buttons*. Along with new Jagger-Richards originals like the whimsical, European waltz-flavoured "Back Street Girl," the psychedelic Bo Diddley-style jam "Please Go Home," "Ride On, Baby" and the acoustic, Appalachian-flavoured "Sittin' on a Fence," the album included their hit singles "Mother's Little Helper" and "Have You Seen Your Mother, Baby, Standing In The Shadow?" along with a cover of Smokey Robinson's "My Girl."

In March of 1967, while on a pleasure trip to Morocco, the delicate fabric of the Stones' interpersonal relationship became frayed even further. Jones had brought along his girlfriend of nearly two years, the beautiful Italian-born model Anita Pallenberg, while Jagger brought his then-girlfriend, singer Marianne Faithfull. When Jones was hospitalized during the trip (for pneumonia), Pallenberg ended up leaving Morocco with Richards. The two soon became romantically involved and would remain together from that point on, which was a telling blow to Jones' fragile ego. And, due to the fact that Pallenberg was subjected to Jones' cruel wit and his chronic episodes of physical abuse, she looked at Keith as her rescuer as well as her paramour. As Richards put it, "Brian's relationship with Anita had reached a jealous stalemate when she refused to give up whatever acting work she was doing to fulfil domestic duties as his full-time geisha, flatterer, punching bag – whatever he imagined, including partaker in orgies, which Anita always resolutely refused to do."

As his destructive relationship with Pallenberg ended, Jones became further estranged from The Rolling Stones, firstly by Andrew Loog Oldham's insistence on emphasising the song writing team of Jagger-Richards on all the albums and secondly by Oldham's decision to focus live performances more on the band's flamboyant and charismatic frontman. This caused Jones to become increasingly anti-social and, occasionally, hostile, although he continued to make key contributions to the band's recordings with his multi-instrumental abilities.

The Stones would close out 1967 by going full-blown into the burgeoning hippie movement with their gaudy psychedelic offering, *Their Satanic Majesties Request*, the only Stones album recorded without a producer (Oldham had finally quit before they began recording in February of that year). Some critics saw *TSMR* as the

Stones' self-indulgent answer to the Beatles' *Sgt. Pepper's Lonely Hearts Club Band*. Even Jagger, in retrospect, dismisses the project as a failure. As Mick told Philip Dodd in *According to the Rolling Stones*: "There's a lot of rubbish on *Satanic Majesties*. Just too much time on our hands, too many drugs, no producer to tell us, 'Enough already, thank you very much, now can we get just get on with this song?' Anyone let loose in the studio will produce stuff like that. There was simply too much hanging around. It's like believing everything you do is great and not having any editing."

During the making of *TSMR*, the Stones put out a quick single on 18 August in the UK and 2 September in the US. "We Love You" (B-side was "Dandelion") would be the final production for Andrew Loog Oldham before he parted ways with the Stones (the official announcement of their split came on 20 September). It's a psychedelic collage of jail sounds, tape-delayed vocal effects and eerie high harmonies from guest background vocalists Paul McCartney and John Lennon. (Jagger and Richards had appeared two months earlier on a filmed version of the Beatles' "All You Need Is Love" shot in London's EMI Studios and broadcast globally via satellite). "We Love You" was written by Jagger-Richards as a response to their 10 May bust for marijuana possession. The tune opens with the sounds of someone entering the jail and a cell door clanging shut, and is quickly followed by Nicky Hopkins' ominous piano riff. It includes the strong anti-establishment lyrics: *We don't care if you hound we and lock the doors around we/you will never win we, your uniforms don't fit we.* The piece trails out on a chorus of horns that bear a strong Moroccan flavour, no doubt influenced by their many visits to Tangier.

TSMR was finally released in December 1967. With its eye-popping 3-D cover that pictured Keith, Mick, Brian, Bill and Charlie dressed up like wizards, mad hatters and Renaissance troubadours seated in front of a mystical palace, *TSMR* definitely stood out in the record bins. But a lot of the material within – the dream-like "In Another Land," written and sung by bassist Bill Wyman, the sprawling hippie jam "Sing This All Together (See What Happens)," the cosmic rocker "2000 Light Years From Home," the spacey "Gomper" and the corny "On with the Show" – was far below the usual Jagger-Richards standard. The one saving grace was the lovely "She's a Rainbow."

If the indulgent *TSMR* was a disappointment, the band would return to form with 1968's *Beggar's Banquet*, which contained such Jagger-Richards masterworks as "Street Fighting Man" and "Sympathy for the Devil," along with blues-soaked originals like "No Expectations" (with Jones on haunting slide guitar), the rootsy "Parachute Woman," the funky "Stray Cat Blues," the countrified "Dear Doctor," the country blues of "Factory Girl" and the stirring, anthemic "Salt of the Earth," sung alternately by Richards and Jagger. Produced by Jimmy Miller, who had previously produced the Spencer Davis Group and Traffic, the Stones' seventh studio album was recorded from March until July and finally released on 8 December 1968 in both the UK (on Decca) and the US (on London), one month after the Beatles' White Album.

Beggar's Banquet was preceded by the 1 June release of the hit single "Jumpin' Jack Flash" (B-side was "Child of the Moon"), another timeless Jagger-Richards original that would continue to appear on the Stones'

concert set lists for the next four decades. Keith described the catchy guitar riff that fuelled "Jumpin' Jack Flash" as the reverse of "Satisfaction," although played on chords instead of just a single-note line. He further called the iconic Stones tune a kind of antidote to the acid-influenced experience of *TSMR*. The first Rolling Stones album on which the song appeared was their 1969 compilation album, *Through the Past, Darkly (Big Hits Vol. 2)*, one year after the single was released. It subsequently appeared on several live Stones albums through the years.

For "Jumpin' Jack Flash," Richards relies on an open D tuning – DADF#AD – which was something he had picked up from Don Everly while on tour in the early days (the Everly Brothers' hits "Bye Bye Love" and "Wake Up Little Susie" used open D tuning). Keith's signature open G tuning five-string tuning, where he removes the lower sixth string and tunes the remaining five to GDGBD, was used on several other Stones numbers, including "Start Me Up," "Brown Sugar," "Tumblin' Dice" and "Honky Tonk Women." Keith explained to *Guitar Player* magazine that he discovered the five-string tuning in early 1969 and has relied on that revolutionary approach ever since for that signature Stones' sound. "The whole idea of getting rid of the sixth string in the open tuning was having the root on the bottom," he told *GP*'s Tom Wheeler in 1983. "You can get a drone going, so you have the effect of two chords playing against each other. One hangs on because you've just got to move one finger – or two at the most – to change the chord, so you've still got the other strings ringing. It's a big sound."

Keith says that learning the five-string open G tuning presented a whole new universe of sound to him and caused him to re-learn the guitar. "It really invigorated me," he said on his website. "It cleared out the clutter. It gave me the licks and laid on the textures."

By 1968, Brian Jones was out of control. While Keith had noticed what he called a cruel, manipulative streak in his bandmate going back to the inception of The Rolling Stones, Jones' complete immersion in alcohol, cocaine, LSD, hashish and amphetamines only exacerbated his evil streak. Jones would appear with the band in December of that year in the movie *The Rolling Stones Rock and Roll Circus*, which also featured The Who, Jethro Tull, Taj Mahal, John Lennon and Yoko Ono. Jones appears drugged in the movie as the band performs raggedy, punk-edged renditions of "Jumpin' Jack Flash," "Sympathy for the Devil" and "No Expectations." His contributions on 1969's *Let it Bleed* were minimal, amounting to playing autoharp on "You Got the Silver" and percussion on "Midnight Rambler." Keith called it "a last flare from a shipwreck."

With his behaviour becoming increasingly erratic – marked by mood swings, motorcycle accidents and various drug convictions which made it impossible for him to obtain a work permit to start an upcoming North

44 Keith Richards holding his favourite Fender Stratocaster, 1988.

46 Mick Jagger with hand drum and Keith Richards with guitar, huddled in the studio with unidentified colleagues during the *Beggars Banquet* sessions, 1968.

50 Striking a pose with Ronnie Wood and The New Barbarians at Madison Square Garden New York, 7 May 1979.

American tour – Jones was approached by Richards, Jagger and Watts on 8 June 1969 and, essentially, forced out of the band he had founded back in 1962. Less than a month later, on 3 July, he was found motionless at the bottom of a swimming pool at his home in East Sussex (he resided in Crotchford Farm which had once belonged to "Winnie the Pooh" author A.A. Milne). He was just 27 years old at the time of his death.

Jones was replaced in The Rolling Stones line-up by 20-year-old former John Mayall's Bluesbreakers guitarist Mick Taylor, who made his first appearance with the band at a free concert in London's Hyde Park two days after Brian Jones' death. They performed in front of an estimated 250,000 fans. The show included the concert debut of their recently-released single, "Honky Tonk Women." Rolling Stones' stage manager Sam Cutler introduced them as "the greatest rock 'n' roll band in the world," a phrase that has stuck to this day.

Richards elaborated on Taylor's presence in the Stones' line-up in a 1977 *Guitar Player* article: "I learned a lot from Mick Taylor, because he is such a beautiful musician. When he was with us, it was a time when there was probably more distinction between rhythm guitar and lead guitar than at any other time in the Stones. The thing with musicians as fluid as Mick Taylor is that it's hard to keep their interest. They get bored – especially in such a necessarily restricted and limited music as rock 'n' roll. That is the whole fascination with rock 'n' roll and blues – the monotony of it, and the limitations of it, and how far you can take those limitations, and still come up with something new."

The Stones concluded their month-long tour of the US in November 1969 with a free concert on 6 December at the Altamont Speedway, just east of San Francisco, that was marked by tragedy. The biker gang Hells Angels provided security for the concert and an audience member near the stage, Meredith Hunter, was stabbed and beaten to death by the gang when they noticed that he was armed. That brutal confrontation was captured in the Albert and David Maysles documentary film, *Gimme Shelter*. In retrospect, Keith called the whole ugly affair at Altamont, "the end of the dream... a culmination of hippie commune and what can happen when it goes wrong."

It was during this highly productive but tumultuous period that Keith began to insulate himself with drugs, heroin being his favorite. And Anita – who on 10 August 1969 had given birth to their son Marlon (named after Marlon Brando) one month after the death of her former lover, Brian Jones – mirrored his voracious appetite for drugs, shooting up as much as three times a day. As Richards told *Rolling Stone* magazine in 1981: "The thing about smack is that you don't have any say in it. It's not your decision anymore. You need the dope, that's the only thing. 'Why? Because I like it.' It takes the decision off your shoulders. You'll go through all those incredible hassles to get it, and think nothing of it. Because that is the number-one priority: first the dope, then you can get home and do anything else that needs doing, like living. If you can. It took me about two years to get addicted. The first two years, I played around with it. It's the greatest seduction in the world."

The Stones' triumphant tour of the States in November 1969, with B.B. King and Ike & Tina Turner as opening acts, was documented on the brilliant live album, *Get Yer Ya-Yas Out!*, which featured much outstanding so-lo work throughout from Taylor, particularly on "Midnight Rambler," "Street Fighting Man" and a galvanizing slide guitar performance on Robert Johnson's "Love in Vain." Keith pulls out his finest Chuck Berry chops on covers of "Carol" and "Little Queenie."

Let It Bleed (released shortly after that 1969 US tour, on 5 December 1969) was Brian Jones' last album with the Stones and the first Stones studio album to feature Mick Taylor. It quickly reached number one in the charts on the strength of such superb Jagger-Richards originals as "Gimme Shelter," "Midnight Rambler" and the glo-rious "You Can't Always Get What You Want." Richards was featured exclusively on lead vocals for the first time on the soulful "You Got the Silver" while Jagger strutted his stuff on the audacious "Monkey Man." "Live With Me" rocked with renewed fervor while they offered something completely different with "Country Honk," an acoustic, countrified take on "Honky Tonk Women" featuring fiddler Byron Berline.

On 6 April 1971, with their contracts having expired with both manager Alan Klein and Decca/London Records, they announced the launching of their Rolling Stones Records imprint and a new association with At-lantic Records. The Stones followed with two platinum-selling albums that many consider to be their best work ever. The first was *Sticky Fingers* (released in the UK on 23 April 1971 and in the US on 30 April). The album featured audacious Andy Warhol cover art that included a working zipper on a jeans-clad male crotch. The mu-sic included some of Jagger-Richards best compositions, including the catchy mega-hit single "Brown Sugar," which Keith largely attributes to Mick, and Richards' soulful minor key ballad, "Wild Horses" (both tunes were recorded at famed Muscle Shoals studios in Sheffield, Alabama during their celebrated 1969 US tour). Richards says that "Wild Horses," like "Satisfaction" before it, "almost wrote itself."

Sticky Fingers also included such memorable Jagger-Richards originals as "Can't You Hear Me Knocking" (with Mick Taylor stretching out on its jazzy coda), the rockin' "Bitch," the overdose anthem "Sister Morphine," the country-twang flavored "Dead Flowers" and a blues-drenched cover of Mississippi Fred McDowell's "You Got To Move."

The bulk of the recording for 1972's excellent double-album *Exile on Main Street*, the Stones' 12th studio al-bum, released in the US on 12 May 1972, was done over a span of one month (7 June – 5 July 1971) in the basement of Keith Richards' rented villa, Nellcôte, in Villefranche-sur-Mer on the French Riviera. That was dur-ing a time when the band members were, literally, in exile, facing an excessive tax burden back home in their native UK. Hence the album title. To this day, Richards regards *Exile* as "maybe the best thing we did."

Exile on Main Street includes such sweaty, visceral Jagger-Richards rockers as "Rip This Joint" and "Rocks Off," the majestic "Tumblin' Dice," the acoustic, countrified "Sweet Virginia" and Richards' "Happy," featuring Keith on lead vocals. They also turn in a slinky take on Slim Harpo's boogie number "Shake Your Hips" along with a cover of Robert Johnson's "Stop Breaking Down."

Keith was in a clinic in Vevey, Switzerland, trying to clean up, when his daughter Dandelion Angela Richards was born in 17 April 1972. (The girl, whom Richards had written the song "Angie" for, was raised by Keith's mother Doris in Dartford, since both of her parents were too drug-addled to care for her). 1973's *Goats Head Soup* (recorded in Kingston, Jamaica) was regarded as 'underwhelming' by critics and fans alike and 1974's *It's Only Rock 'n Roll*, sparked by the energized title track, was considered by skeptics to be the Stones' 'comeback' album.

Following Mick Taylor's departure from the Rolling Stones in December 1974, former Jeff Beck Group and Faces guitarist Ronnie Wood participated in the band's March 1975 recording sessions for their forthcoming album, *Black and Blue*. Former Canned Heat guitarist Harvey Mandel also participated in those sessions. As Richards told *Guitar Player* in a 1977 interview: "After Mick Taylor left, we rehearsed for about six months with a lot of good guitar players from all over the world. And we could work with them, you know, and they could work with us. But when Ronnie became available and suddenly walked in, that was it. There was no doubt. It was easy. It was much harder to get a Rolling Stones sound with Mick Taylor. It was much more lead and rhythm, one way or the other. As fabulous as he is as a lead guitarist, he wasn't as great as a rhythm player, so we ended up taking roles. When Brian and I started, it was never like that. It's much easier than with Brian, personally. But also with Ron, the basic way we play is much more similar, and this isn't in any way to knock Mick. I mean, he's a fantastic guitar player. But even if he couldn't play shit, I'd love the guy. But chemically we didn't have that flexibility in the band. It was, 'You do this, and I'll do that, and never the twain shall meet.' With Ron, if he drops his pick, then I can play his lick until he picks it up, and you can't even tell the difference."

While still a member of the Faces, Wood toured with the Stones on their "Tour of the Americas '75" from 1 June to 8 August. The tour, which kicked off in New York City with the Stones performing on a flatbed trailer being pulled down Broadway, featured stage props including a giant inflatable penis and a rope on which Jagger swung out over the audience. Wood officially became a member of the Rolling Stones in December of 1975.

During the decadent mid 1970s, the Stones embraced a glam aesthetic while Mick flaunted androgynous sexuality and Keith indulged in hardcore narcotics. And their reputation preceded them on their tours of the US, where charges of corrupting young America and inciting youth to rebellion followed them. They were, in fact, branded by the U.S. State Department as "the most dangerous rock-and-roll band in the world," even though Richards considered himself and his mates "mere minstrels."

From 10-12 January, Keith was tried in London for possession of LSD and cocaine. He was found not guilty of the LSD charge but guilty of the cocaine charge and given a fine. His response: "Why don't they pick on the Sex Pistols?" Richards was busted again, this time in Toronto on 24 February 1977, for narcotics possession and trafficking. It took 19 months from the arrest to the trial in October 1978. Richards was ultimately exonerated from the charge that could have landed him in jail for years.

The heroin, the cocaine, the booze, the women, the violence and petty cruelties, the dangerous gun play backstage, the car wrecks, the irresponsible ditching of duties in the middle of recording sessions to inexplicably run off to Jamaica ... it was all a part of living the rock 'n' roll lifestyle during the tumultuous 1970s.

It was around that time that his relationship with Anita Pallenberg began melting down. Her slide into narcotics caused her to become delusional, paranoid and self-destructive, sometimes accompanied by bursts of rage, generally hurled at Keith or at their son Marlon. He likened her behavior during that dark period to Hitler's. The situation had become unbearable. Breakup was imminent.

Following their separation, Pallenberg took a new lover (17-year-old Scott Cantrell). Tragically, the boy shot and killed himself while playing Russian roulette with a gun in Richards' house while Keith was away in Paris. Anita was cleared of any charges of involvement in the boy's death and, soon after, she and Marlon moved to New York. In her new life, Pallenberg became immersed in a crazy hipster scene centred around the Mudd Club, CBGBs and Max's Kansas City and including such figures as artists Andy Warhol and Jean-Michel Basquiat, art dealer Robert Fraser, novelist-poet William Burroughs as well as punk bands like the Dead Boys and the New York Dolls. Meanwhile, the Stones kept rolling along, continuing their multi-platinum-selling ways with 1978's *Some Girls* (featuring the punk-edged "Shattered," the rockin' "Respectable," the decadent "When the Whip Comes Down," the soulful "Beast of Burden" and the discofied "Miss You," underscored by Sugar Blue's harmonica). They followed with 1980's *Emotional Rescue* featuring Mick's falsetto vocals on the title track and Keith's gravelly vocals on his "All About You" and 1981's *Tattoo You*, with Keith's super-charged, opening guitar riff from "Start Me Up" setting the tone for the album and Sonny Rollins' tenor sax solo on the mellow "Waiting on a Friend" taking the band to a whole new place.

For a change of pace, Richards participated in an off-shoot project in 1979 dubbed The New Barbarians, featuring Return To Forever bassist Stanley Clarke, The Meters drummer Zigaboo Modeliste, Ian McLagan on piano and organ, long-time Stones sideman Bobby Keys (who had played a key role on *Exile on Main Street*) on saxophone and Keith's Stones bandmate Ronnie Wood on second guitar and pedal steel guitar. Wood actually served as bandleader for that tour, put together to promote his 1979 solo album *Gimme Some Neck* (which Richards, Charlie Watts and Mick Taylor also played on). Together they toured the US from 24 April – 22 May, performing loose, rambunctious versions of Wood originals from *Gimme Some Neck* like "Infekshun," "Buried Alive" and "F.U.C. Her" along with covers of Chuck Berry's "Sweet Little Rock 'n' Roller," B.B. King's "Rock Me Baby," Bob Dylan's "Seven Days" and Stones tunes like "Honky Tonk Women" and "Jumpin' Jack Flash." At their Chicago appearance, blues legend Junior Wells sat in on harmonica and vocals on "Key to the Highway." The New Barbarians also performed two charity concerts in Toronto, fulfilling one of the conditions of Richards' 1978 sentence for heroin possession. Keith loved playing concerts with The New Barbarians. Freed from the responsibility of Stones tours, he loosened up and had a ball as the hired gun on that tour.

Looking ahead, the real challenge for Keith and his partner/adversary Mick became how to hold The Rolling Stones together while growing old gracefully through the 1980s, 1990s and beyond.

56-57 The Rolling Stones posing for a publicity photo, circa 1965. From left to right: Bill Wyman, Charlie Watts, Mick Jagger, Keith Richards and Brian Jones.

58-59 Brian Jones, Mick Jagger and
Keith Richards travelling by train during
their 1965 European tour.

60 Keith, surrounded by fans, at Heathrow airport at the height of the British Invasion, 23 June 1966.

61 The Stones strutting their stuff at the peak of their popularity in the mid 1960s, en route to a month-long US tour, 23 June 1966.

62-63 With Brian Jones, whom Richards thought cruel and manipulative with a fragile ego, at the height of their audacious sartorial splendour, 1967, during a press conference.

64 and 65 Mobbed by female fans in Manchester, 11 March 1965, following recording of ITV's "Scene at 6:30" show.

66 and 67 Young and baby-faced at
the piano and in repose at the New York
Hilton, 28 October 1965.

68 In a rare moment of repose with cigar on the set of *The Rolling Stones' Rock And Roll Circus*, Intertel Studios, Stonebridge Park, 11 December 1968.

69 On the set of *The Rolling Stones' Rock And Roll Circus*, 11 December 1968. From left to right: Pete Townshend, John Lennon, Yoko Ono, Keith Richards, Charlie Watts, Mick Jagger, Brian Jones, Bill Wyman and Eric Clapton.

70 The Rolling Stones at the Kensington Gore Hotel in London, posing for publicity shots for *Beggars Banquet*, 5 December 1968.

FOLLOWING THE INDULGENT *THEIR SATANIC MAJESTIES REQUEST*, **THE ROLLING STONES WOULD RETURN TO** FORM ON 1968'S *BEGGAR'S BANQUET*, WHICH CONTAINED SUCH **JAGGER-RICHARDS MASTERWORKS** AS "STREET FIGHTING MAN" AND "SYMPATHY FOR THE DEVIL."

72 Strikingly beautiful Italian-born model-actress Anita Pallenberg and her romantic partner Keith Richards relaxing at home, December 1969.

73 With Anita Pallenberg at home, De-

74-75 Anita and Keith with newborn son Marlon outside King's College Hospital in Dulwich, London, 10 August 1969.

76 Keith Richards of the Rolling

MARLONRICHARDS

RAISED ON CHUCK BERRY RIFFS AND BO DIDDLEY BEATS, **RICHARDS EMULATED HIS EARLY R&B AND BLUES INFLUENCES** BEFORE FINDING HIS OWN VOICE AS A SONGWRITER.

78 Warming up at a rehearsal with trusty Gibson Les Paul Custom guitar prior to a concert at the Saville Theatre in London, 15 December 1969.

79 With Mick in the studio, June 1969.

80 With members of the production crew relaxing on the Stones' private jet with a friendly game of cards, circa 1970.

A QUINTESSENTIAL ROCK 'N' ROLL ROAD WARRIOR, **KEITH CLAIMS TO HAVE SLEPT ONLY TWICE A WEEK** DURING HIS EARLY YEARS WITH THE ROLLING STONES.

82 and 82-83 With Anita Pallenberg and their young children Marlon and Angela, circa 1974 (left) and two years later (1976).

84 At Heathrow airport met by Anita Pallenberg and four-month old son Marlon, December 1969.

85 With his son Marlon at Schiphol airport in Amsterdam, October 1970.

86 Carrying his son Marlon while on a break from The Rolling Stones, March 1971.

86-87 Carrying his son Marlon and followed by Anita Pallenberg at their hotel in Newcastle upon Tyne, March 1971.

88 With son Marlon at his home, the rented Villa Nellcôte, a 19th century, sixteen-room mansion on the waterfront at Villefranche-sur-Mer on the Cote d'Azur where the band recorded *Exile on Main Street*, April 1971.

89 During a break from recording *Exile on Main Street* in the basement of Keith's rented Villa Nellcôte on the Cote d'Azur, with Anita Pallenberg playing in the backyard with their son Marlon, April 1971.

90 Holding his son Marlon up above him during a sound check at The Empire Pool, Wembley, London, September 1973.

90-91 Playing drums during a sound check as his son Marlon looks on, The Empire Pool, Wembley, London, September 1973.

92 An interview at Atlantic Records in London, August 1974.

93 Posing for a portrait, circa 1974.

94 and 95 An interview at Atlantic Records in London, 1974.

96 Tuning a new Fender Telecaster for a sound check during The Rolling Stones' US tour, 1975.

97 Relaxing backstage with a prized 1953 blonde Fender Telecaster guitar (note capo at the sixth fret), 1975.

98-99 Relaxing at the bar in 1980 with favourite beverage, Jack Daniel's on the rocks.

99 On tour with The New Barbarians in 1979. His constant companion, a bottle of Jack Daniel's.

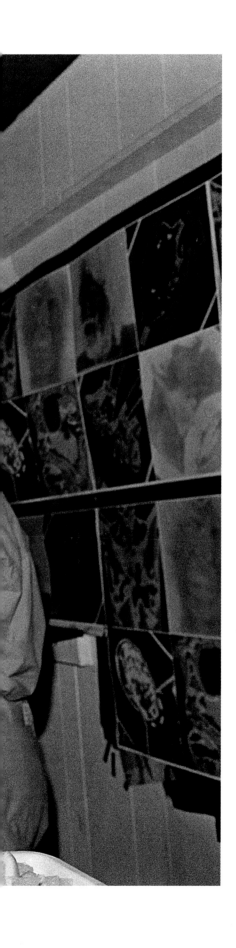

100 Posing in upstate New York, shortly after his arrest in Toronto for heroin possession, 1978.

101 In his luxurious rented villa, Nellcôte, in Villefranche-sur-Mer, near Nice, where the Rolling Stones recorded *Exile*

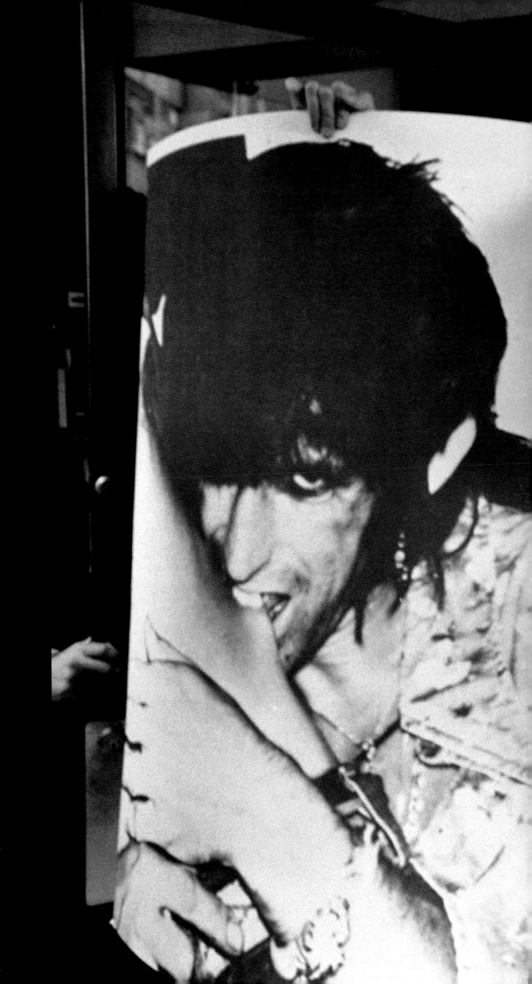

102-103 The Rolling Stones (minus Keith Richards) at the Marquee Club in London for the launch of *Love You Live* (1977).

104 With former Faces guitarist Ronnie Wood, recruited to The Rolling Stones in 1975, enjoying a moment of backstage jamming before taking to the stage.

105 On tour in 1979 with The New Bar-barians (from left to right: Ronnie Wood, drummer Zigaboo Modeliste, keyboardist Ian McLagan, bassist Stanley Clarke, Keith Richards).

106-107 With Ronnie Wood cooling out in a small commuter plane, 1979.

108-109 Saxophonist Bobby Keys (left), Keith Richards and Ronnie Wood with The New Barbarians in concert in Madison, Wisconsin, 1 January 1979.

109 With Ronnie Wood in the Hal Ashby film *The Rolling Stones: Let's Spend the Night Together*, documenting the band's 1981 US tour.

110 Performing during a concert at the Oshawa Civic Auditorium in Toronto, Canada, circa 1979.

111 On stage with The New Barbarians at New York's Madison Square Garden, 7 May 1979.

KEITH'S DIRECT, **INCISIVE AND INVENTIVE GUITAR RIFFS** DEFINED ICONIC ROLLING STONES TUNES.

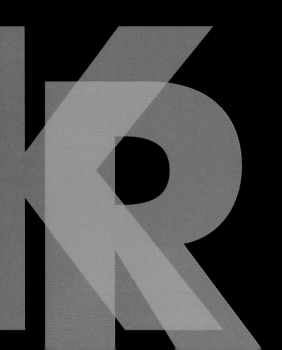

112 With Mick Jagger performing on stage at the Oshawa Civic Auditorium in Toronto, Canada, playing a benefit concert after Keith Richards' drug bust, 22 April 1979.

113 With Ronnie Wood in concert with The New Barbarians, an off-shoot band formed by Wood that featured bassist Stanley Clarke, keyboardist Ian McLagan and drummer Zigaboo Modeliste, at New York's Madison Square Garden, 7 May 1979.

114-115 Performing with The New Barbarians at New York's Madison Square Garden, 7 May 1979.

116 Performing with The New Barbarians, 1979.

117 Playing a Travis Bean guitar with The New Barbarians, 1979.

Rock 'n' Roll Lifer

STILL RIFFING AFTER ALL THESE YEARS

It was 17 March, Saint Patrick's Day, 1979 that Keith first laid eyes on model Patti Hansen. He had gone to New York's Studio 54 disco, ostensibly to avoid Swedish actress, former James Bond girl and onetime Rod Stewart girlfriend Britt Ekland who, reputedly, had the 'hots' for the Stones guitarist and was pursuing him all over town. Keith figured Studio 54 was the unlikeliest place to find him, so he hid out there with The Mamas and Papas founder (and fellow druggie) John Phillips. On the dance floor he spotted Patti, who happened to be celebrating her 23rd birthday with friends that night at Studio 54. Hansen was strictly high profile at the time, pictured on the covers of *Vogue*, *Esquire*, and *Harper's Bazaar* magazines. The face of Calvin Klein Jeans, she even had a traffic-stopping billboard in Times Square, which Keith, no doubt, had seen on numerous occasions.

The successor of supermodels Cheryl Tiegs and Farah Fawcett, she was later called "the Marilyn Monroe of the '80s" by no less than renowned fashion photographer Francesco Scavullo. And, although she was certainly aware of The Rolling Stones, she probably didn't know Keith Richards from Keith Moon. But he was mesmerized by her, and the vision of Patti dancing wildly, with hair flying, stayed with him for the next eight months until they met again, this time at Keith's 36th birthday celebration on 18 December at the Roxy roller disco in New York. Keith's manager Jane Rose had been following Hansen's progress in the fashion mags over the year and made sure to formally invite her to Keith's birthday bash. It was there, at the Roxy, that the seeds of romance were planted.

By January 1980, Richards had written in his diary: "Incredibly, I've found a woman. A miracle! I've pussy at the snap of a finger but I've met a woman! Unbelievably she is the most beautiful (physically) specimen in the WORLD. But that ain't it! It certainly helps but it's her mind, her joy of life and (wonders) she thinks this battered junkie is the guy she loves. I'm over the moon and peeing in my pants. She loves soul music and reggae, in fact everything. I make her tapes of music, which is almost as good as being with her. I send them like love letters. I'm kicking 40 and besotted."

Keith began wooing Patti quite relentlessly after that. He'd take her to nightclubs, like Tramp's, to see his favorite bands or up to Harlem in search of rare blues and R&B records. He'd send her witty love letters and drawings done in his own blood. And it was all so spontaneous and fresh and exciting to her. By March 1980, Richards had moved into Hansen's Greenwich Village apartment. Their relationship grew tighter that year, having survived a disastrous Thanksgiving at her parents' home on Staten Island (Keith showed up drunk with a bottle of Jack Daniels and his acoustic guitar, which he later smashed on the dinner table in a fit of rage). But they weathered the ups and downs and painful separations – he would invariably go out on tour with the Stones, she would, occasionally, take on a movie project that took her out of town – and stayed together.

While Keith's new relationship with Patti may have been in the ascendance, his 'marriage' to Mick Jagger was showing signs of discord. As saxophonist Bobby Keys, who worked on 1980's *Emotional Rescue,* noted, "It seemed like Keith and Mick were a little bit more polarized on that session. There wasn't quite the same vibe when everyone was gathered together as there had been in the *Exile On Main Street* days."

It was in Paris, while working on *Emotional Rescue* at Pathéé Marconi Studios, that Keith finally realized he had kicked his heroin habit. He had been given a free bag of smack at a dinner with friends and ended up throwing it in the street on his way back to the hotel afterwards. "That's when I realized I was no longer a junkie," he writes in 'Life.' "Even though I'd been basically off the stuff for two or three years, the fact that I could do that meant I was out of its power."

Mick and Keith spent a lot of 1981 in meetings, discussing ways in which they could resolve their differences and get the Stones back on the road. In August, a month before they kicked off their US promotional tour for *Tattoo You* , the members of the Stones held a band meeting to discuss the upcoming tour and also to warn Ron Wood that he would have to curb his cocaine habit if he wanted to join them. The subsequent tour was a roaring success, culminating in a concert in Hampton, Virginia on Keith's 38th birthday on 18 December, after which the Stones went their separate ways – Mick, Charlie Watts and Bill Wyman flying to France, Keith and Ron Wood returning to England.

In February 1982, Keith spent time in Los Angeles with comedian John Belushi a few weeks before the former *Saturday Night Live* and *Animal House* icon's tragic death from overdosing on a speedball (a potent mixture of heroin and speed) at the famous Chateau Marmont in Los Angeles. In May, the Stones reconvened to begin month-long rehearsals for their 1982 European tour, which commenced on 2 June and concluded on 25 July, the eve of Mick's 39th birthday. Later in the year, Mick and Keith met in Paris to begin working on demos for *Undercover* (the first Rolling Stones album to be distributed by CBS Records). But the rift between Jagger and Richards seemed to widen during these sessions. According to Keith, Mick had started to become unbearable in his need to control everything, giving the rest of the Stones a feeling of being subordinate 'hirelings' rather than equals in the band. As Richards put it at the time, "As far as he was concerned, it was Mick Jagger and *them*."

Keith further describes the tense atmosphere, during the *Undercover* sessions, as hostile and discordant, marked by a bare minimum of talking and some occasional bickering. The album also reflects Jagger's disproportionate influence in the Jagger-Richards writing team, particularly on tunes like the politically-charged title track, "Tie You Up (The Pain of Love)," "Too Much Blood" and "She Was Hot." But Richards was complimentary about his partner's contributions. As he said at the time: "I think Mick has done an incredible job. I think he's taken quite a leap forward, lyric-wise, on this album."

Outside the Stones' bubble, Richards was still madly in love with Patti Hansen. They had been together for four years by December 1983. Wanting to "make this thing more legitimate," he wed Patti on his 40th birthday (18 December 1983). The ceremony took place in Cabo San Lucas, Mexico, with Mick as Keith's best man. Within a few years, Keith had a second family — daughter Theodora was born in 1985 and Alexandra came along the following year.

Following the release of the disjointed *Undercover*, Jagger parted ranks with the Stones in 1984 to focus on a solo album, *She's the Boss*, which featured one Jagger-Richards song, "Lonely at the Top," although Richards himself did not appear on the album as guitarist (that spot was capably filled by the likes of Jeff Beck, Pete Townshend and Carlos Alomar). Feeling that the Stones should be the first priority, Keith was not pleased by Mick's pursuance of solo work. And yet, unbeknownst to the rest of the Stones, Jagger had signed a multi-million dollar deal with CBS to deliver three solo records. Keith felt it was a tacky move by Jagger and he spoke for the rest of the group in feeling betrayed by Mick's behind-the-back maneuvering.

From that point on, friction between the two life-long friends, who, by now, shared the joint-producer pseudonym The Glimmer Twins on Stones album credits, only increased. Their carefree boyhood days of scouring London record shops together in search of obscure blues records were now far behind them. They had arrived at a point where their relationship was strictly business, which, during his most reflective moods, Keith regretted when he spoke of missing his dear old friend. Nevertheless, Keith and Mick continued to plug away as the prodigious song writing team that they had been since the mid 1960s. Meeting up in January 1985, they tried to rekindle that magic once again on *Dirty Work* . But, conflict remained part of the fabric of their relationship. The sessions were delayed because Mick was finishing up his solo album, *She's the Boss*, which only aggravated Keith further. Predictably, the atmosphere for those *Dirty Work* sessions was charged with bad vibes.

When the album was released in March 1986, it contained only three Jagger-Richards compositions ("Hold Back," "Winning Ugly" and "Sleep Tonight"), the fewest since 1965's *Out of Our Heads*. As Keith said at the time: "I would think that at least half the album will be Jagger-Richards-Wood. There's no doubt about it, mainly because Mick was very busy on his own." Added Ron Wood: "Mick and Keith were at a low writing ebb and they gladly accepted my songs."

And when Jagger refused to tour to promote *Dirty Work*, explaining that he wanted to get on with his solo career, it only infuriated Richards. "We'd be idiots not to tour," he said at the time. "We've got a good album

WHEN A REPORTER ASKED RICHARDS, "WHEN ARE YOU AND MICK GOING TO STOP BITCHING AT EACH OTHER?" KEITH REPLIED

here! It'd be the dumbest move in the world not to get behind it. We spent a year making it and putting our backs to the wall. Why toss it away?"

When Jagger later told a London tabloid that The Rolling Stones were a millstone around his neck, the rift between himself and Richards escalated to a level that Keith referred to as "World War III." For him, the unforgivable betrayal came when Mick announced in March 1987 that he would go on a tour with his own band to promote his second solo album, *Primitive Cool*. It was a slap in the face for Richards, who was outraged and hurt by Jagger's selfish actions, which only spurred speculation that the Stones had indeed come to the end of the road. When a reporter asked Richards at the time, "When are you two going to stop bitching at each other?" Keith replied, "Ask the bitch."

On 16 October 1986, Richards participated in two gala concerts at the Fox Theater in St. Louis in celebration of Chuck Berry's 60th birthday. The event was filmed (including some revealing backstage footage) and, eventually, released the following year as the Taylor Hackford documentary, *Hail! Hail Rock 'n' Roll*. On drums for that gala concert was Steve Jordan, whom Richards had worked with earlier in 1986, on Aretha Franklin's recording of "Jumpin' Jack Flash," for the soundtrack of a Whoopi Goldberg movie of the same name, released in October 1986. Keith originally intended to have Charlie Watts on drums for that Chuck Berry tribute, but the Stones drummer was fighting his own battle with narcotics at the time. Richards replaced him with Jordan, who was a perfect foil for Keith's rhythmic sensibility.

Still feeling the sting of rejection at what he perceived as Mick's desertion from the Stones, Keith responded by beginning work on his own solo album during the summer of 1987, at the same time that Mick was going out on tour with his own band. Working closely with Jordan, who became his new writing partner, Richards worked on demo sessions in early April. By July, he had signed a contract with Virgin Records. Jagger's *Primitive Cool* was released on 11 September, around the same time that Keith began recording tracks for *Talk Is Cheap* at Le Studio in Montreal.

Keith's solo debut was released on 3 October 1987 to critical acclaim. Along with strong, no-frills offerings like the classic riff-oriented rocker "Take It So Hard" (the album's promotional single), "Whip It Up," "Big Enough," the Al Green-flavoured "Make No Mistake" and the lovely, emotionally charged "Locked Away," *Talk Is Cheap* included "You Don't Move Me," which was slyly aimed at his Stones partner Mick.

118 Life-long blues hound posing with a Blind Willie McTell album, circa 2000.

120 Studio portrait of 59-year-old Keith Richards, circa 2002.

124 Posing in photographer's studio, circa 1981.

Keith began rehearsals in early November 1987 with his X-Pensive Winos band, featuring drummer Jordan, guitarist Waddy Wachtel, saxophonist Bobby Keys (who had played such a key role on *Exile on Main Street*), keyboardist Ivan Neville and bassist Charley Drayton. Their *Talk Is Cheap* tour commenced on 24 November at Atlanta's Fox Theater, where Richards had performed the year before with Chuck Berry for the *Hail! Hail Rock 'n' Roll* concert documentary. Richards' first solo tour concluded on 17 December at the Brendan Byrne Arena in East Rutherford, New Jersey, raising the question of whether or not The Rolling Stones would ever get back together.

"Mick and I are still sort of testing each other at this point," he told *Pulse* magazine during the *Talk Is Cheap* tour. "But I love the guy. I love to work with him. There are certain things about what he's done that piss me off, but nothing more than what goes down with any friends, really. If you can't lean on your mate then you're not really his friend, right? Then you're an acquaintance, not a friend. Mick and I go a little bit beyond just being able to insult each other. I mean, we've known each other for 40 years. It's not just two rich superstars indulging in a power struggle. It's about us trying to find each other at this point. And I think at this point, Mick is probably realising that he really needs The Rolling Stones more than actually The Rolling Stones need Mick."

On 18 January 1988, The Rolling Stones were inducted into the Rock 'N' Roll Hall of Fame in a ceremony at the Waldorf-Astoria Hotel in Manhattan. It was their first public appearance together since early 1986. For the end-of-ceremony jam they were joined onstage (sans Bill Wyman and Charlie Watts) by Stevie Wonder, Tina Turner, Little Richard, The Temptations and Pete Townshend, performing "Satisfaction," "Honky Tonk Women" and "Start Me Up."

Committed to starting the band up again, Mick and Keith agreed to convene in Barbados in mid-January 1988 to discuss working on the first new Stones album in five years. In March, they were joined by Charlie Watts, Bill Wyman and Ron Wood to begin demo-ing new material for what would become *Steel Wheels*. Recording began at Air Studios in Montserrat on 31 March 31 and continued until 2 May. In mid-June, Keith, Mick and Ron Wood travelled to Tangier to record the Master Musicians of Jajouka for the exotic song "Continental Drift."

Critical response to *Steel Wheels* was generally positive. As *Rolling Stone* magazine's Anthony DeCurtis wrote: "Nothing reinvigorates Sixties icons like having something to prove. In the past few years the reverence typically shown both The Rolling Stones and Bob Dylan has worn perilously thin. The Stones' last two albums, *Undercover* and *Dirty Work* – not to mention Mick Jagger's solo recordings – ranged from bad to ordinary, and Keith Richards's bitter public baiting of Jagger suggested that this particular twain might never again productively meet. Now, in the summit of love of the past, the Stones and Dylan have weighed in with albums that signal renewed conviction and reactivated sense of purpose. *Steel Wheels* rocks with a fervour that renders the Stones' North American tour an enticing prospect indeed."

The Stones concluded their year-long Steel Wheels World Tour on 24 August 1990 with the two concerts at London's Wembley Stadium that were filmed for an IMAX movie (*At The Max* was released at IMAX theatres around the world on 25 October that year). Those concerts marked Bill Wyman's last appearances with The Rolling Stones. At the time, Richards commented, "I always said that nobody leaves this band except in a coffin. But he made up his mind... sometimes people get to the end of their tether."

In 1991, Keith made guest appearances on albums by John Lee Hooker (*Mr. Lucky*), Tom Waits (*Bone Machine*) and Johnnie Johnson (*Johnnie B. Bad*). And by March 1992, he had begun work on material for his second solo album. Recording with his X-Pensive Winos continued through the summer. When *Main Offender* was finally released on 20 October, it was hailed by critics as being as focused and stripped-down as *Talk Is Cheap*, typified by such catchy raunch 'n' roll numbers as "Wicked as It Seems," "Eileen," "Bodytalks," "Will But You Won't" and the searing "999." In November, the X-Pensive Winos followed up with the band's first European tour.

In April 1993, Jagger and Richards convened at their usual meeting place in Barbados to begin discussing and working on the next Stones album. By now, the Glimmer Twins had learned to live with their disagreements, like an old married couple. But the creative spark between them was still evident. Demo sessions for this new Stones' project started in May. In June, Mick and Keith auditioned bass players, at S.I.R. Studios in New York, to fill Bill Wyman's shoes (they ended up hiring former Miles Davis and Sting bassist Darryl Jones). Full band rehearsals took place through the month of July in Ron Wood's home studio in Ireland. Recording began in early September, and continued on and off through December, in London and Dublin (around the time of Keith's 50th birthday) with Don Was (of the group Was Not Was) producing.

Overdubbing and mixing sessions continued in January, February and March, and *Voodoo Lounge* (their first album in nearly five years) was finally released on 11 July 1994. The album was hailed as fierce, fundamental roots rock 'n' roll, akin to *Beggars Banquet*. Critics singled out such potent Jagger-Richard originals as "You Got Me Rocking," "I Go Wild," "Sparks Will Fly," the hyper-charged "Mean Disposition" and the countrified "Blinded By Rainbows." And in his rare lead vocalist role with the Stones, Richards showed a soulful touch on the more sedate, introspective ballads "Thru and Thru" and "The Worst."

The subsequent Voodoo Lounge World Tour was another year-long affair that raked in record profits. Keith closed out 1995 by recording with a group of Rastafarian musicians and friends at his home in Point of View, Jamaica for the album *Wingless Angels* (which wouldn't be released until November 1997).

In July, 1996, Richards fulfilled a longstanding dream by recording a song ("Deuce and a Quarter") at Levon Helm's home studio in Woodstock with guitarist Scotty Moore and drummer D. J. Fontana (Elvis Presley's sidemen on his early 1950s rockabilly sides for Sun Records) for the Elvis tribute album *All the King's Men*. While feeling humbled in such regal company, Keith, nonetheless, held his own on the session with his unaffected, no-nonsense licks.

Later that year, in October, he met with Mick and Ron Wood to discuss undertaking a new album and tour. They began working on demos in London, in December, continuing the process at the end of January 1997 in New York. Sessions for *Bridges to Babylon* began on 13 March at Ocean Way Studios in Los Angeles and continued there, after a break in April, until July. To promote the album and tour, they drove across New York's Brooklyn Bridge in a red Cadillac on their way to a press conference. Co-produced by Don Was, The Glimmer Twins and the Dust Brothers, *Bridges to Babylon* included the Jagger-Richards composition "How Can I Stop," which Richards calls "one of the best Rolling Stones songs ever" and which featured a brilliant solo from legendary jazz saxophonist Wayne Shorter. Richards also contributed the tune "Thief in the Night," which he co-wrote with his guitar tech Pierre du Beauport.

Regardless of its luke-warm critical reception, the subsequent Bridges to Babylon World Tour confirmed the Stones' status as one of the strongest live acts. The European leg of the tour, which was to kick off in May in Berlin, was delayed for nearly a month after Keith fell off a ladder in his library at home in Connecticut, resulting in a punctured lung. (A year later, Keith punctured his other lung and broke three ribs in a fall at his home in St. Thomas in the Virgin Islands).

By the end of 1998, the Stones had given their first performance in Russia, at Moscow's Luzhniki Stadium, while also performing their first-ever concert in Turkey. On 2 November, their seventh live album, *No Security*, was released. Their lengthy world tour continued until June 1999.

The year 2000 marked some highs and lows for Keith, who accomplished a couple of personal projects. In April, he recorded with guitarist Hubert Sumlin, long-time sideman to blues legend Howlin' Wolf, and, in July, he was reunited with his one-time love from the first Stones tour in 1964, singer Ronnie Spector, for a recording session in New York City. But tragedy struck on 30 August, when his father, Bert, passed away at the age of 85.

The following year, Keith appeared on the Grammy-winning Hank Williams tribute album *Timeless*, which included performances by Bob Dylan, Tom Petty, Mark Knopfler, Sheryl Crow and Johnny Cash. Keith recorded his track, a version of Hank's bluesy ballad from 1952, "You Win Again," at his home in Connecticut with Les Paul's rhythm guitarist (Lou Pallo) and bassist (Paul Nowinski) along with drummer George Recile.

Following the tragic destruction of the World Trade Center on 11 September 2001 and the massive loss of life from that terrorist attack, Mick and Keith appeared at the nationally-televised all-star benefit "The Concert for New York City" at Madison Square Garden on 20 October, performing "Salt of the Earth" and "Miss You" to an audience of first responders from the New York Fire Department and New York Police Department and those who had been involved in the rescue and recovery efforts at Ground Zero.

From late February until early March of 2002, Mick and Keith worked on demos at Richards' home in Ocho Rios, Jamaica, for The Rolling Stones' upcoming recording sessions. By that summer, they released their double-album greatest hits package *Forty Licks* to mark their 40th anniversary as a band.

In October 2002, Richards again played sideman to his boyhood hero, former Howlin' Wolf guitarist Hubert Sumlin, on *About Them Shoes*. Keith played on two tracks, sharing guitar chores on Sumlin's slow blues "This Is the End, Little Girl" and also on a mesmerizing, dirge-like interpretation of the Muddy Waters tune "Still a Fool" the latter featuring Keith on gruff, earthy vocals in keeping with the Chicago blues tradition. Hubert was 73 at the time of the record's ultimate release in January 2005. (When Sumlin passed away on 4 December 2011 at the age of 80, Keith and Mick picked up the full expenses for the bluesman's funeral).

Bassist Nowinski, who also participated in those sessions for *About Them Shoes*, describes his connection with The Rolling Stones' ace guitarist: "I met Keith in 1999 when he came down to the Les Paul gig back at the old Iridium nightclub in New York. I was Les' regular bassist at the time. Les always had a strict policy of not allowing people to hang out during a sound check but one day I noticed this elderly woman sitting there... and this is hours before the show started. Nobody knew who it was. Turned out it was Keith's mom. She came down because she didn't believe that Keith actually knew Les Paul, so she showed up early. Keith finally showed up for the second set with his entourage and he got up and played, which was pretty fun, as you can imagine. Then after the gig he said to me, 'Hey, would you ever want to come over to my house and jam in Connecticut?' And of course I was like, 'Sure, any time.' So I gave him my number and I didn't hear anything for a long time. A year later I got a call from Keith, and I started going up there about three days a week. It was just me, Keith, Blondie Chapman and George Recile. They were all closer, older friends and they were into just hanging with Keith. And after a few times of jamming up there, Keith invited me to stay over. That continued for about a two and a half year period, and there was a tremendous amount of recorded material from those sessions that is in the can. I have 18 CDs full of unfinished tracks that are incredible. And the thing that was funny about that whole experience was, it was almost like with your first band, where you're just down in the basement jamming. It was basically a finished basement. That's what Studio L was, it was like an L-shaped basement, and that's where we'd just be hanging out."

"We had gear set up and I had my little cubby-hole next to a closet where I stood with my upright bass. The drums were in another room next to the pool table. But basically, the drums were never being used. Keith would make George play on cardboard boxes because he was trying to keep it real soft. And I remember Keith having this very fancy old Neumann microphone that was supposed to be worth something like $35,000 dollars. So we'd all huddle around this mic and just play tunes. And there was never any discussion of what we were going to play. We'd just play songs until something would happen. It was just a process of hashing stuff out in Keith's basement."

"And one day Hubert Sumlin showed up. Keith adored Hubert. He was just excited to be down there in his L-shaped basement, hanging out with Hubert. Hubert is the coolest, sweetest guy of all time and Keith's really the same way... just a great cat. So they were just hanging and talking and they got along so well. And, with that song we did, 'Little Girl,' we were just sitting around when they started playing. I picked up my bass and all of a sudden they had to rush to move the mics to the right spot to capture the moment. It was very, very off-the-cuff. As usual, there was never a plan. There was never a discussion about what we were going to play. Keith would never tell anybody what to do ever. I never heard a word out of his mouth directing anybody."

In November 2003, a four DVD set chronicling The Stones' Forty Licks World Tour (including their first-ever concerts in India and China) was released. Turning 60 on 18 December that year put Keith in a reflective mood regarding the Stones' future. "Can it be done?" he wondered at the time. "Can you actually be a rock 'n' roller for this long? I played with cats who were just as powerful the day before they died, Muddy Waters being one. It remains to be seen if that will hold true for either Mick or myself."

By early June 2004, Keith was back plotting out another album with his life-long writing partner Mick, this time at Jagger's home studio, La Fourchette, in Pocéé sur Cisse, France. Demos were completed by September and by early December 2004 the Stones had started recording *A Bigger Bang*, their first full studio album since 1997's *Bridges to Babylon*. Sessions at Jagger's La Fourchette studio were completed by April and in June they held overdubbing and mixing sessions at Los Angeles' Ocean Way Recording Studios, site of countless class rock 'n' roll sessions since the 1970s.

It was in June 2005 that Richards began hanging out in Los Angeles with actor Johnny Depp. It would prove to be the beginning of a tight friendship between the two enigmatic superstars. Depp, who had modeled his Captain Jack Sparrow character, from *Pirates of the Caribbean,* on Richards, tried to persuade Keith to join the lucrative movie franchise. The idea was to cast the Stones' guitarist as the gruff Captain Teague, Captain Jack's long-lost father, for the filming of *Pirates of the Caribbean: Dead Mans' Chest*. As the shooting schedule conflicted with a Stones tour, Keith turned down the offer. But he did, eventually, make a cameo appearance as the Captain Teague in 2007's *Pirates of the Caribbean: At World's End*. (As he jokingly commented at the time, "After a lifetime of playing the blues, I'm going to be remembered as a fucking pirate!").

A Bigger Bang was finally released on 3 September 2005 and was followed by the usual exhaustive US tour, which concluded on 5 February 2006 with a half-time show at Superbowl XL at Ford Field in Detroit. As Keith noted at the time: "Quite honestly, I don't like American football. I think it's a spectacle, not a sport. When you've got the team on the run, you don't give 'em time out for a bloody ad. But the NFL is sort of that icon thing. It's fun but I don't consider that Superbowl performance to be any sort of major highlight of my career."

131 Shooting a sly smile for the camera, 1990.

On 27 April 2006, Keith suffered a serious injury after falling from a tree while on holiday in Fiji and cracking his skull, which resulted in brain surgery in nearby New Zealand. "Everyone imagines it was a fifty-foot-tall palm tree," he said at the time. "It's embarrassing, really. I was sitting on this gnarled shrub about six feet off the ground. I was wet – I'd been swimming. I hit the ground the wrong way, my head hit the trunk and that was that. It's not the first brush with death I've had. I guess what I learned is, don't sit in trees anymore."

Richards returned to Stones tour duty on 11 July after recuperating for a month and a half. On 29 October, they played the first of two special concerts at the intimate Beacon Theater in New York City, both of which were filmed by Martin Scorsese, who had used the Stones' "Jumpin' Jack Flash" in his 1973 film *Mean Streets* and "Gimme Shelter" for the climactic scene in his 1990 film, *Goodfellas*. The gala event included guest appearances by Jack White of the White Stripes (on "Shine A Light"), Christina Aguilera (on "Live with Me") and blues guitar legend Buddy Guy (on Muddy Waters' "Champagne & Reefer"). Former President Bill Clinton and his wife, Senator Hillary Clinton, were in attendance for the show.

While on a break from the Stones' A Bigger Bang World Tour in 2007, Richards participated in Stones' saxophonist Tim Ries' solo recording, *Stones Project II*. An adventurous two-CD set (recorded for Ries' own Tames Music Group and licensed to the Sunnyside label), Reis' exotic Stones' tribute album featured an array of musicians from around the world recording on their home turf, including Portuguese fado singer Ana Moura ("No Expectations," "Brown Sugar"), Japanese vocalist Minako Yoshida and guitarist Kazumi Watanabe ("Baby Break It Down") and the North African Tuareg band Tidawt ("Hey Negrita"). Stones drummer Charlie Watts appeared on a lightly swinging jazz-waltz rendition of "Miss You," recorded in Paris, Richards provided his signature guitar licks on a soulful rendition of "Baby Break It Down," recorded in Tokyo, and Mick Jagger blew some mean blues harp alongside Ronnie Wood's lap-steel guitar work on the entrancing "Hey Negrita."

In March 2007, Richards inducted The Ronettes at the annual Rock and Roll Hall of Fame award ceremonies at the Waldorf Astoria in New York City. Then, in April, he flew to England to be at the bedside of his mother Doris as she passed away at the age of 91 on 1 May. More bad news came that year when Keith's wife Patti Hansen, who had already survived a breast cancer scare in 2005, discovered she had bladder cancer. "The breast cancer was nothing compared to the bladder cancer," she told *Harper's Bazaar*. Since underwent immediate surgery and follow-up chemotherapy and has been cancer free since. She continues to work with New York's Memorial Sloan-Kettering Cancer Center at raising awareness for the disease.

Keith also grabbed headlines in 2007 for a remark he made to a British tabloid journalist. In the story, he had mentioned that after his father's death in 2002 and subsequent cremation, he mourned his passing by snorting his ashes. While some declared that Keith had gone too far this time, others suggested the ingestion of an ancestor was actually an accepted ritual going back to ancient times. Regardless, the news stirred up a storm of controversy around the world.

The Stones' 2007 A Bigger Bang European Tour was highlighted by their first-ever appearance at the Isle of Wight Festival in Newport, England, where Amy Winehouse guested with them. In June, they released another four-DVD documentary set entitled *The Biggest Bang*, featuring concert performances from across their 2005-2006 tour. By late July, Keith had signed a deal with publisher Little Brown to write his autobiography, due for release in 2010.

The Stones A Bigger Bang World Tour concluded on 27 August 2007 with three concerts at the O2 Arena in London, making it the longest and most extensive tour of their career and the highest grossing in rock history. The final tally on that two-year international tour was $558 million, which placed the Stones in the Guinness Book of World Records.

The following year, 2008, saw the release of the Martin Scorsese-directed Rolling Stones concert film *Shine A Light*, which was shown in both regular cinema theatres and IMAX theatres worldwide and, subsequently, released as a DVD. Two years later, in 2010, Keith, Mick and Charlie Watts attended the premiere of the documentary film *Stones in Exile* at the Museum of Modern Art in New York City. Directed by Stephen Kijak, who pieced together vintage footage from the band's intensive 1971 *Exile on Main Street* sessions in the basement of Richards' rented villa in the South of France, *Stones in Exile* premiered at the Cannes Film Festival and was subsequently released on DVD in June.

By early October 2010, the Stones saw the release of the restored concert documentary DVD *Ladies and Gentlemen, The Rolling Stones*. But Keith's crowning achievement came at the end of that month – the release of his disarmingly frank autobiography, 'Life,' which was published to wide acclaim, ultimately winning the Norman Mailer Award (presented to him at a gala ceremony, on 8 November in New York, by former President Clinton). In her Amazon.com review of the book, Daphne Durham wrote: "Richards is as comfortable in his bones as a worn pair of boots, and 'Life captures the rhythm of his voice so effortlessly that reading his tale is like sharing a pint with an old friend – one who happens to be one of the most iconic guitarists of all time."

In his *New York Times* review of 'Life,' Michiko Kakutani wrote: "By turns earnest and wicked, sweet and sarcastic and unsparing, Mr. Richards writes with uncommon candour and immediacy... He gives us an indelible, time-capsule feel for the madness that was life on the road with the Stones in the years before and after Altamont; harrowing accounts of his many close shaves and narrow escapes (from the police, prison time, drug hell); and a heap of sharp-edged snapshots of friends and colleagues... But 'Life' is way more than a revealing showbiz memoir. It is also a high-def, high-velocity portrait of the era when rock 'n' roll came of age, a raw report from deep inside the counterculture maelstrom of how that music swept like a tsunami over Britain and the United States. It's an eye-opening all-nighter in the studio with a master craftsman disclosing the alchemical secrets of his art."

Given his uncomplimentary comments in the book about his partner, and Jagger's rather defensive reaction to Keith's scathing comments, it remains to be seen whether The Glimmer Twins will ever get back together to revive the Stones once again. "I'm trying to nail them down but I don't want to crucify them!" Keith says. "Something's blowing in the wind. The idea's there. We kind of know we should do it, but nobody's put their finger on the moment yet. We can, if Mick and Charlie feel like I do, that we can still turn people on. We don't have to prove nothing anymore. I just love playing, and I miss the crowd."

Meanwhile, Richards has been hard at work with drummer-collaborator Steve Jordan, preparing new material for an upcoming solo release. As bassist Paul Nowinski reports: "Keith and Steve blocked out Germano Studios on 3rd Street for about six months and they went to work at it every day. About a week before Christmas, 2010, I got a call from Keith's manager Jane Rose asking if I was in town and available. I was doing the Hugh Jackman show on Broadway at the time and was pretty flexible during the day. So I came by and we did a nice track. I just overdubbed on some stuff. And I actually did a whole viola da gamba session where I stacked up a whole string section, which was pretty fun. Keith had originally gotten me into the whole viola da gamba thing ten years ago, and when I was out touring with Rickie Lee Jones I found a gamba on the road and just started fucking around with it. So I ended up doing a whole string section on one of their tunes with it, which was definitely an experience. Keith had said, 'Can you come and play the gamba on this track?' And I was like, 'Man, I'm not a professional gamba player but I'll try.' So I was sitting there and was kind of nervous and Keith was massaging my shoulders saying, 'Take it easy, you're gonna be OK.' And two hours later we had a finished whole orchestral string gamba section on this tune they had been working on. It was cool."

Like so many others who have worked with Richards over the years, Nowinski reveals that The Rolling Stones' iconic guitarist is actually far more down-to-earth than those outside the Stones bubble can possibly imagine. "Obviously, he's one of the biggest stars in the business but he's a totally mellow person. It's like the most surprising thing. He's just a cool guy. He's got like zero ego. I love playing with him."

Nowinski also confides that on his last session with Richards, he learned an important lesson that will last a lifetime. "I remember being bummed out because I had played something I thought was a mistake and I thought I screwed up the entire track. I think it was on 'You and Again.' It was just one note. And Keith said to me, 'Paul, all of my best things I've ever done is when I've made the right mistake.' And that really stuck with me.

"He's the greatest," added Nowinski. "He's like one of the most well-rounded musicians that I know. One time when I was up at his place in Connecticut, we woke up and Keith had prepared this big English breakfast – bangers and mash and whatever. And while he was making breakfast he was listening to Vivaldi's mandolin concertos for guitar. And after he finished making the eggs he picked up this acoustic guitar that was next to the stove and he began playing the slow movement of the Vivaldi concerto exactly perfectly along with the record.

He played the whole thing by ear, and he played it beautiful. That guy... he's got more music in him than people know. I think he can do anything. What can you say? He's a for-real guy."

After half a century of rocking and rolling, Richards has surpassed the age that his boyhood hero, Muddy Waters, was at the time of his passing in 1983. Now a grandfather, he proudly presides over family gatherings during holidays and special occasions. His son Marlon, by all accounts a polite, witty and gentlemanly vegetarian, has three young children of his own – son Orson and daughters Ella and Ida – with his wife, the former Yves St. Laurent model Lucie de la Falaise. Daughter Dandelion (she now goes by her middle name Angela) resides in an estate just two miles up the road from Daddy's house in Redlands. Their mother, Anita Pallenberg lives in a farmhouse nearby.

Keith's two grown daughters by Patti Hansen, Alexandra and Theodora, are both rising star models living in Manhattan. Alexandra caused a bit of stir in 2010 by posing nude for French *Playboy*. But as she told the British *Daily Express* tabloid at the time, "When I was approached I laughed with my mum, who did *Playboy* in the past. I am young and when I get older I can look back at that and say I have done it. I worked my butt off in the gym to get in shape for this shoot so why not show off?" Alexandra also works as a DJ in New York City nightclubs. Her sister Theodora, who is studying painting and drawing, made headlines in March 2011 after being arrested for writing graffiti on a convent wall in New York City. When the police stopped her, she had marijuana and another controlled substance in her possession.

"I love my families," said patriarch Richards. "I have several extended families and they all love each other. I'm extremely blessed with my ladies who all, thank God, get along."

And while some might suggest that Keith has not aged gracefully – putdowns range from "prehistoric reptile" to "degenerate street person" – there is no denying that he is the ultimate rock 'n' roll survivor. Writer Hillary Johnson opined in her Style & Culture column for the *Los Angeles Times*: "Richards looks like he's been staked to an ant hill in the Gobi desert for the last 40 years and is proud of his status as an unrepentant and unreformed libertine. If there really were an island of lost boys, this is what their leader would look like after six decades of fun and games. Richards wears his elephant hide with pride, as wilfully ugly inside as he is out. Because of his strange failure to mature, Richards' ravaged face and body are as fascinating to gaze upon as a ten-car pileup. You can't help looking, because there but for the grace of God go you."

Indeed. But as the contented elder statesman or rock 'n' roll told *People* magazine: "Getting old is a fascinating thing. The older you get, the older you want to get."

Still hungry for new challenges and excited about the music-making process after all these years, Keith is now fully engaged in a life-long journey of self-discovery. As he told *Rolling Stone*: "To me, the main thing about living on this planet is to know who the hell you are and be real about it. That's the reason I'm still alive."

136-137 Model Patti Hansen embraces her boyfriend Keith Richards, circa 1981.

139 In a cloud of smoke, displaying his skull ring, circa 1981.

140 Performing with The Rolling Stones in concert at Candlestick Park in San Francisco, California on 18 October 1981.

141 Sporting a cannabis necklace in concert with the Stones, 1982.

BY JANUARY 1980, RICHARDS FOUND LOVE AGAIN WITH MODEL PATTI HANSEN.

HE WROTE IN HIS DIARY: "INCREDIBLY, I'VE FOUND A WOMAN. A MIRACLE! SHE THINKS THIS BATTERED JUNKIE IS THE GUY SHE LOVES. I'M KICKING 40 AND BESOTTED."

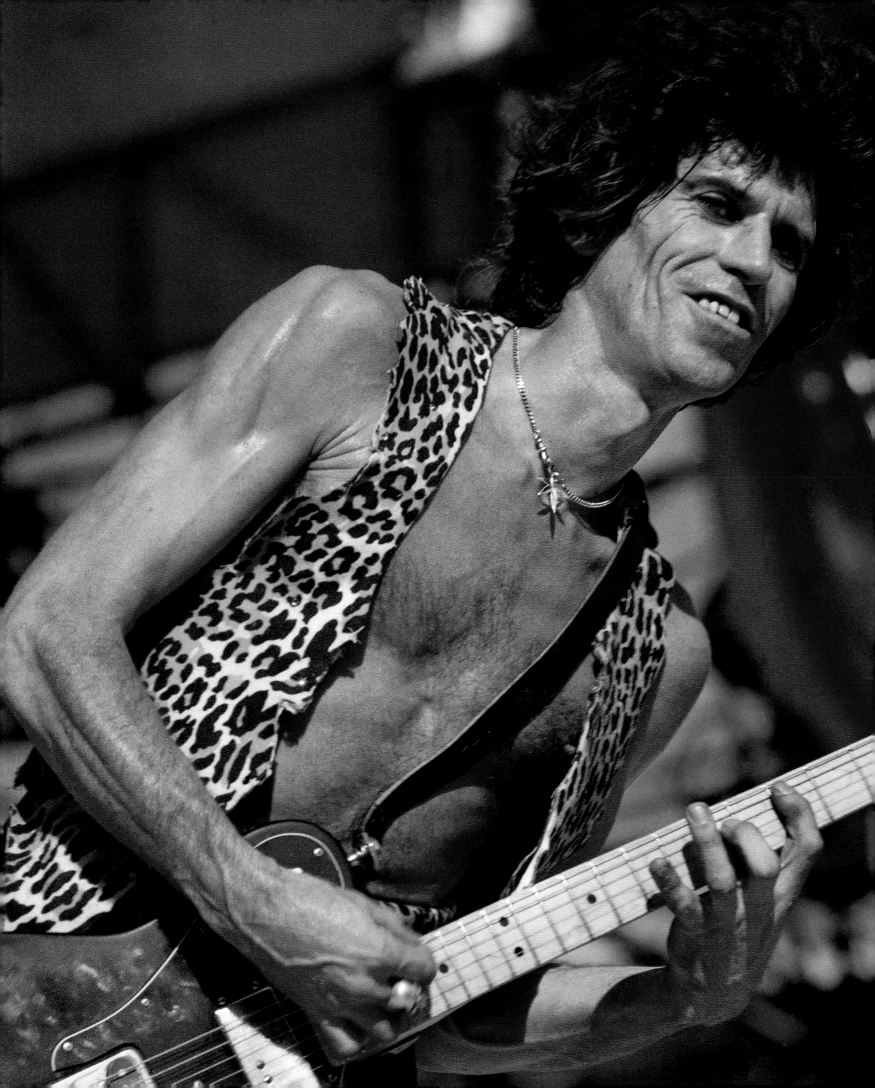

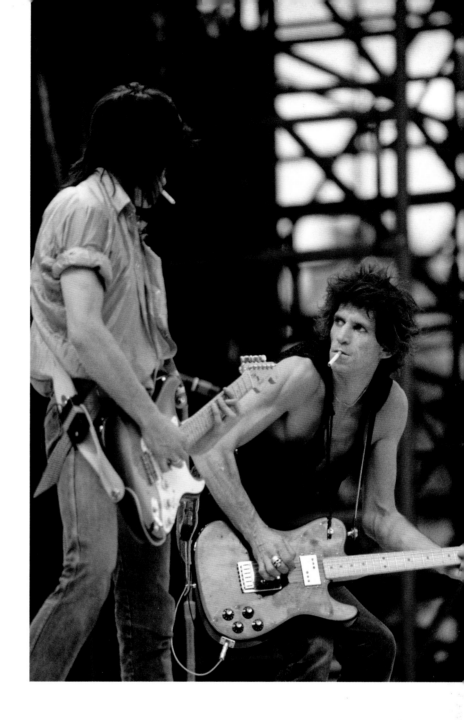

142-143 Keith Richards rarely took the role of lead singer with The Rolling Stones. His first featured vocal spot was on "Happy" from 1972's *Exile on Main Street*. It became a regular part of their set lists over the next three decades. Richards is pictured here singing and trading licks with Stones bandmate Ronnie Wood during a concert at Folsom Field in Boulder, Colorado, October 1981.

143 Ron Wood and Keith Richards playing and smoking during a concert at Folsom Field in Boulder, Colorado, October 1981.

144 and 145 Performing with The Rolling Stones, circa 1982.

146-147 Yet another smoking portrait, circa 1982.

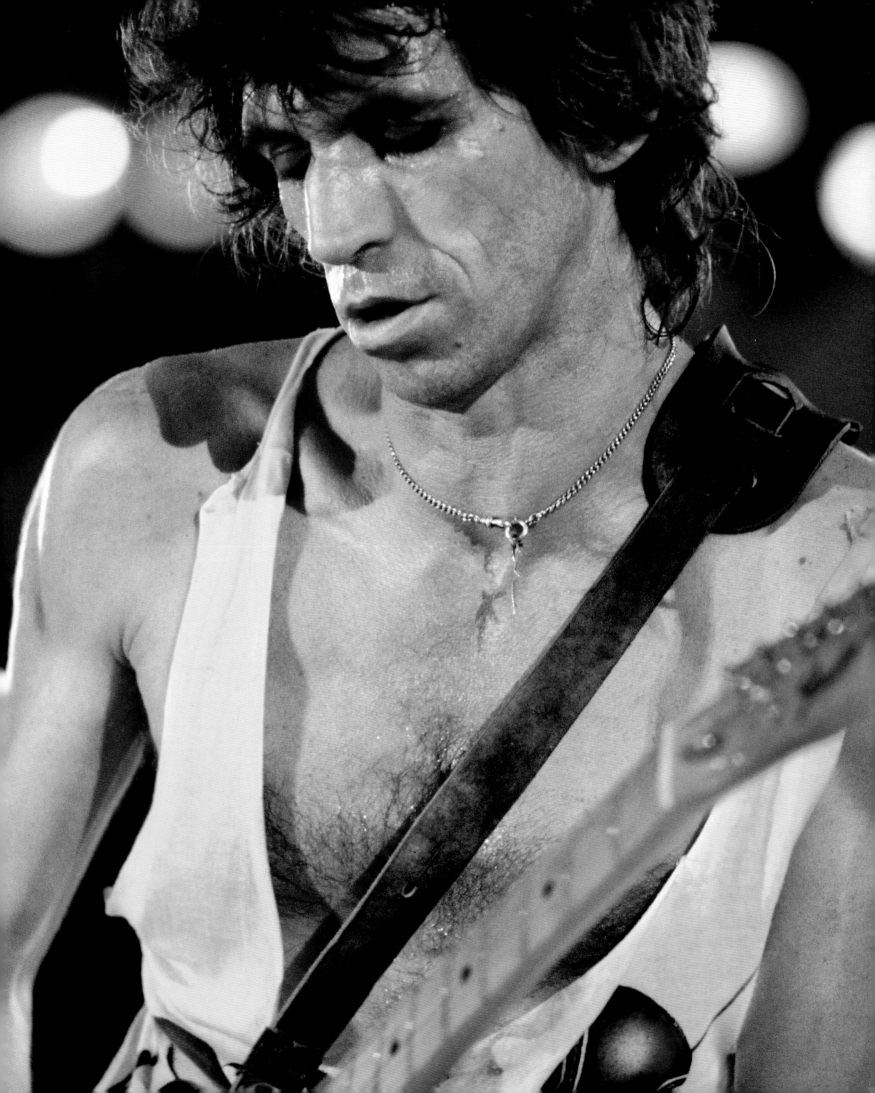

148-149 Richards with cannabis necklace, skull ring and black eye liner, circa 1982.

150 Close-up for the camera, circa 1990.

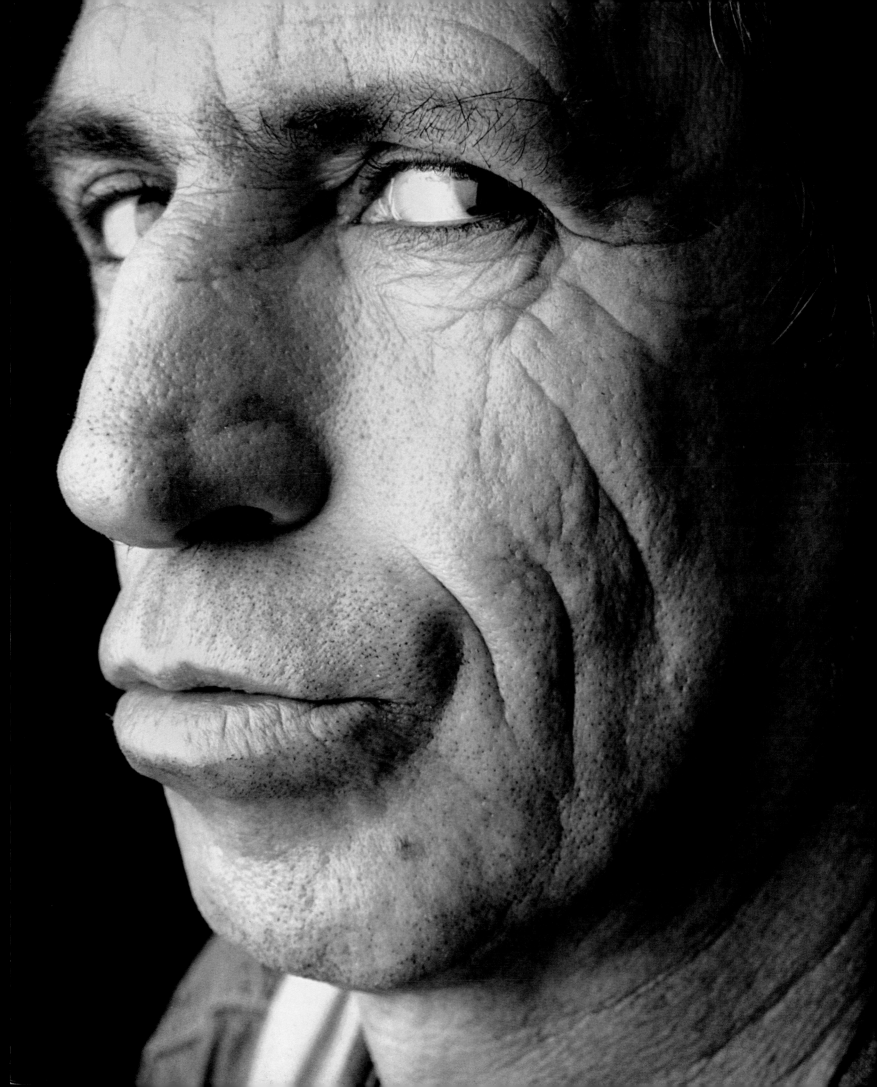

HE'S BEEN JAILED, PILLORIED IN BRITISH TABLOIDS, HOSPITALIZED AND ON THE BRINK OF DEATH ON AT LEAST A FEW OCCASIONS. AND YET, HE IS STILL HERE.

KEITHRICHARDS

152-153 The ravaged face of a rock 'n' roll warrior, Rolling Stones guitarist Keith Richards, circa 2010.

154 In concert with the Stones in Syracuse, New York, 1982.

155 On the Stones' Steel Wheels Tour in Jacksonville, Florida, 1989.

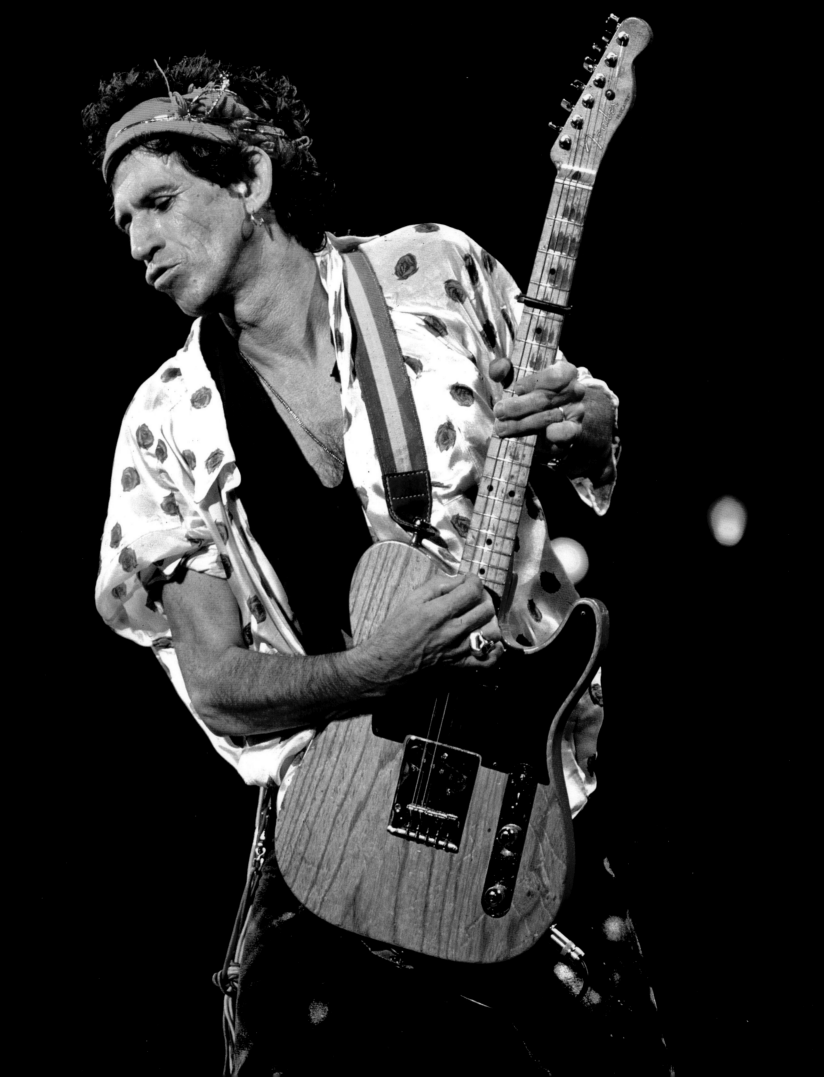

156 Colourfully garbed and dancing with his favourite axe during The Rolling Stones' Steel Wheels Tour, 1989.

157 Striking a dramatic rock star pose with his trusty 1953 blonde Fender Telecaster on the Stones' 1989 Steel Wheels Tour.

158-159 Ronnie Wood and Keith Richards on The Rolling Stones' Steel Wheels Tour in Atlantic City, New Jersey, 1989.

160-161 Posing in photographer's studio around the time of his solo debut, 1988's *Talk is Cheap*.

162-163 In the comfort of his Connecticut home, relaxing with his 1964 Martin acoustic guitar in his octagonal library around the time of his second solo release, 1992's *Main Offender*.

164 In concert during the Main Offender Tour of America, 1993.

165 Riffing in concert with X-Pensive Wino bassist Charley Drayton, 1993.

166-167 Ron Wood (with Gibson Firebird guitar) and Keith Richards (with Gibson Les Paul Junior guitar) during 1994's Voodoo Lounge Tour.

KEITHRICHARDS

STILL RIFFING AFTER ALL THESE YEARS STILL RIFFING AFTER ALL THESE YEARS

168-169 Singing and playing (Fender Telecaster) with backup singers and The Rolling Stones, mid 1980s.

170 At home in Connecticut, circa 2000.

A LARGER-THAN-LIFE ROCK STAR AND BONA FIDE GUITAR HERO, **KEITH WAS NAMED #4** IN *ROLLING STONE* MAGAZINE'S LIST OF 100 GREATEST GUITARISTS OF ALL TIME.

KEITHRICHARDS

172 The lion in winter at his Connecticut home, circa 2000.

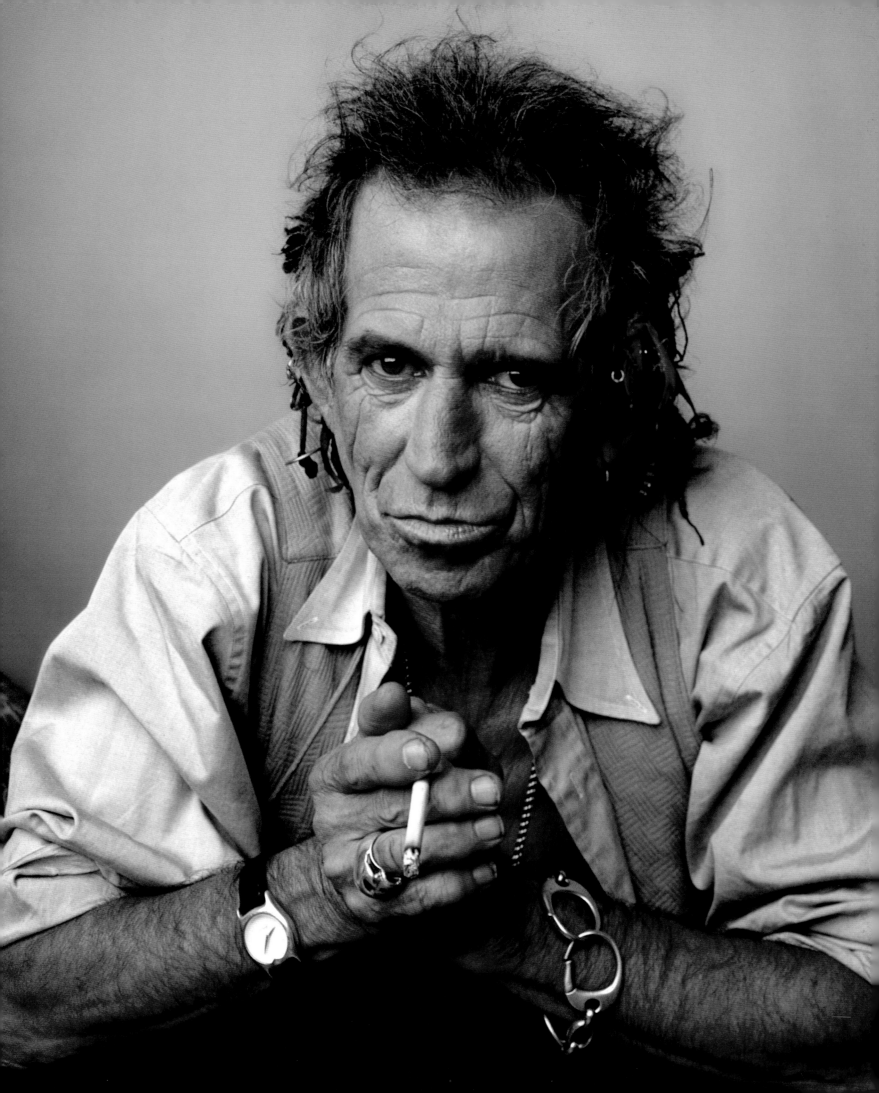

174-175 The aging rock icon in repose at age 59, circa 2002.

176-177 In his rococo music room in his Connecticut home, circa 2000.

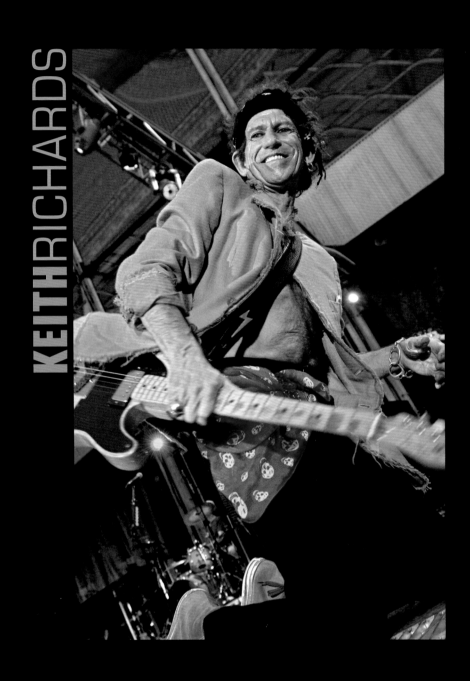

180 and 181 On stage at the Stade de France in Saint-Denis near Paris during the band's Forty Licks Tour, 9 July 2003.

182-183 Striking a dramatic pose (with his 1975 black Telecaster Custom) on stage alongside his lifelong song writing partner Mick Jagger during a Rolling Stones concert at Petco Park in San Diego, 14 November 2005.

184-185 Rolling Stones frontmen Mick Jagger and Keith Richards enjoy a happy moment together in their ongoing love/hate relationship 10 May 2005

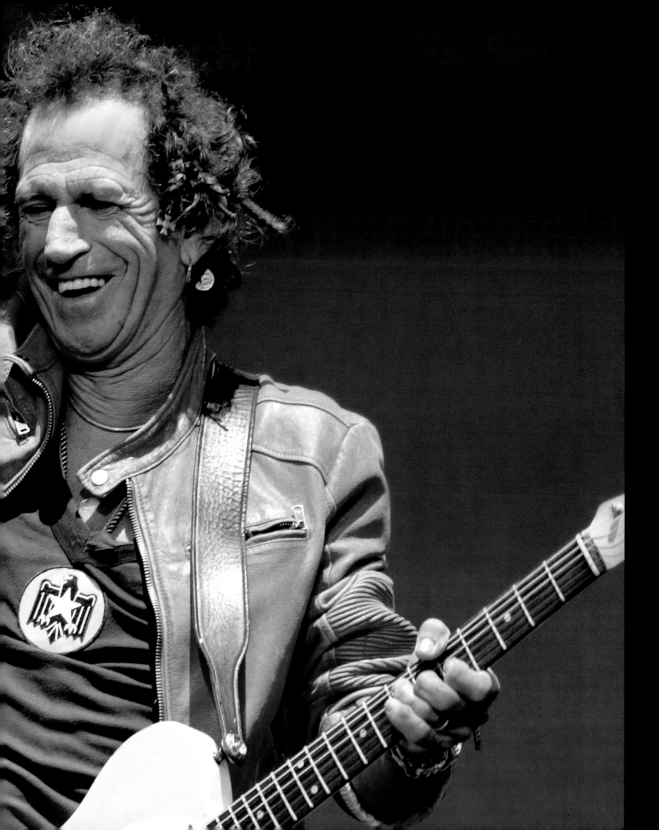

"REALLY. IF YOU CAN'T LEAN ON YOUR MATE THEN YOU'RE NOT REALLY HIS FRIEND, RIGHT?"

186 and 187 Playing during The Rolling Stones concert at Dodger Stadium in Los Angeles, 22 November 2006.

188-189 With his 1959 black Gibson ES-355 guitar and The Rolling Stones performing during the half-time show of Super Bowl XL in Detroit, Michigan, 5 February 2006.

190-191 Performing during the half-time show of the Super Bowl XL between the Pittsburgh Steelers and Seattle Seahawks at Ford Field in Detroit, Michigan on 5 February 2006.

"CHUCK GOT IT FROM T-BONE WALKER, AND I GOT IT FROM CHUCK, MUDDY WATERS, ELMORE JAMES AND B.B. WE'RE ALL PART OF THIS FAMILY THAT BACK THOUSANDS OF YEARS. REALLY, ALL PASSING IT ON."

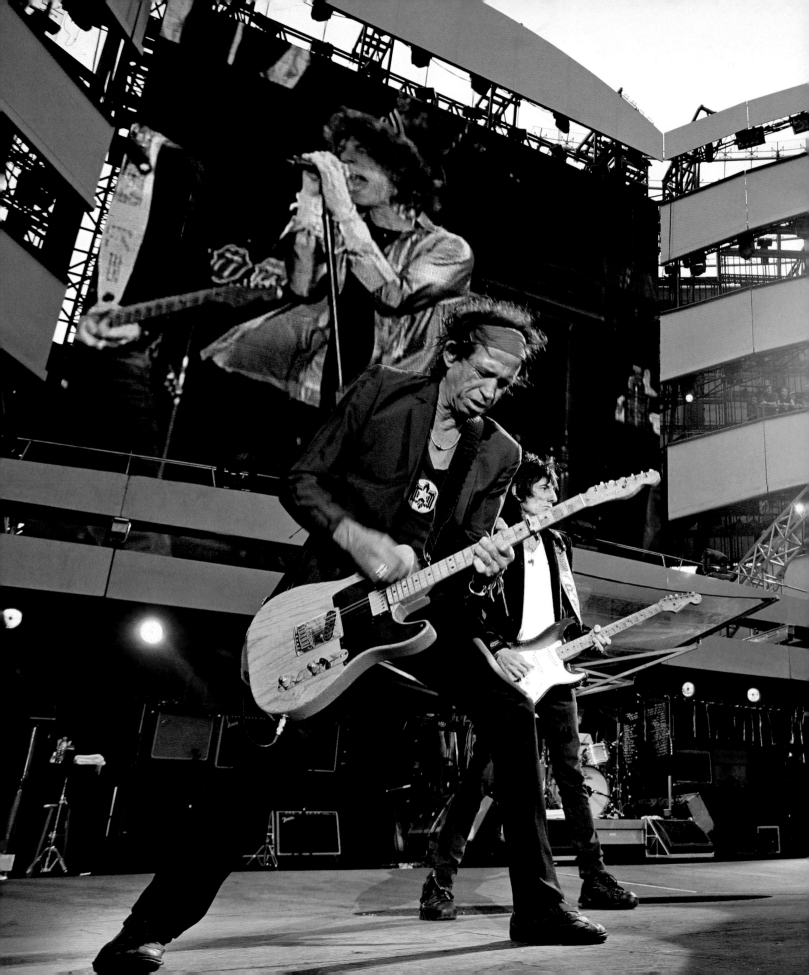

192-193 The Rolling Stones (from left to right: Keith Richards, Ronnie Wood, Mick Jagger) on stage at Berlin's Olympic Stadium, 21 July 2006.

194-195 and 195 With his 1975 black Fender Telecaster Custom in concert with The Rolling Stones in Amsterdam, Netherlands, 31 July 2006.

197 In concert in Bucharest, Romania during The Rolling Stones' A Bigger Bang European Tour, 17 July 2007.

"KEITH WROTE TWO-AND THREE-NOTE THEMES THAT WERE MORE POWERFUL THAN ANY GREAT SOLO. **THERE WAS AN EMOTIONAL CONTENT THAT SPOKE TO ME.**" — NILS LOFGREN

198 Movie poster for the 2008 Martin Scorsese documentary on The Rolling Stones, *Shine A Light*.

198-199 The Rolling Stones (Ronnie Wood, Charlie Watts, Mick Jagger and Keith Richards) pose with director Martin Scorsese (centre) during Paramount Pictures' press conference for *Shine A Light* at the New York Palace Hotel, circa 2008.

200-201 Attending a book signing for his autobiography, "Life," at Waterstone's bookstore in London's Piccadilly Circus, 3 November 2010.

202 and 202-203 Decked out in full Captain Teague regalia for his cameo appearance in 2011's *Pirates of the Caribbean: On Stranger Tides*.

204 With his wife Patti Hansen arriving at the world premiere of *Pirates Of The Caribbean: On Stranger Tides* at Disneyland on 7 May 2011 in Anaheim, California.

"GETTING OLD IS A FASCINATING THING. **THE OLDER YOU GET, THE OLDER YOU WANT TO GET.**"

AUTHORS

VALERIA MANFERTO DE FABIANIS. Born in Vercelli, Italy, Valeria Manferto De Fabianis received her high school diploma in classical studies and then pursued studies of a literary character, receiving a degree in philosophy at the Università Cattolica del Sacro Cuore in Milan. Passionate about travel and nature, she has collaborated in producing television documentaries and various reportage for the most prestigious specialized magazines in Italy. An expert in photo editing and image creation, she has also supervised the drafting of texts for numerous photographic volumes. In 1984, together with Marcello Bertinetti, she founded Edizioni White Star, becoming editorial manager. Worthy of special note among her accomplishments are the successful CubeBook series; *Fidel Castro. El Líder Máximo: A Life in Pictures*; *John Lennon. In His Life*; *Fur and Feathers: An Unusual Farm*; *Lingerie*; *A Matter of Style: Intimate Portraits of 10 Women Who Changed Fashion*; and *Rolling Stones. 50 Years of Rock*. She has conceived and curated photographic exhibitions meeting with success in various major cities both in Italy and abroad.

BILL MILKOWSKI is a Manhattan-based freelance writer who contributes to several music publications, including *Jazz Times, Jazziz, Absolute Sound, Jazzthing* (Germany), *Guitar Club* (Italy) and *Guitar* (Japan). His writing has also appeared in *Down Beat, Guitar Player, Bass Player, Acoustic Guitar, Pulse!, MIX* and *Interview*. He is also a consultant for Wolfgang's Vault, a website that streams historic concerts from the Newport Jazz Festival archives (available atwww.wolfgangsvault.com. He is the author of *JACO: The Extraordinary and Tragic Life of Jaco Pastorius; Swing It! An Annotated History of Jive; Rockers, Jazzbos & Visionaries; Legends of Jazz* (Edizioni White Star, 2010). In 2011, he co-authored *Here And Now! The Autobiography of Pat Martino*. Milkowski has written over 500 sets of liner notes and produced records for the Blue Note, Columbia, JVC and NYC Records labels. In 2004, he received the Helen Oakley Dance-Robert Palmer Award for Excellence in Newspaper, Magazine, Online Feature or Review Writing from the Jazz Journalists Association and in 2011 received a Lifetime Achievement Award from the JJA.

PHOTO CREDITS

KEITHRICHARDS

A DAVID & CHARLES BOOK
F&W Media International Ltd 2012

David & Charles is an imprint of F&W Media International, Ltd
Brunel House, Forde Close, Newton Abbot, TQ12 4PU, UK

F&W Media International, Ltd is a subsidiary of F+W Media, Inc.,
10151 Carver Road, Cincinnati OH45242, USA

© White Star Publishers,
Via Candido Sassone, 24
13100 Vercelli, Italia
www.whitestar.it

First published in the UK in 2012

ISBN-13: 978-1-4463-0255-2
ISBN-10: 1-4463-0255-5

Printed in China for:
F&W Media International, Ltd
Brunel House, Forde Close, Newton Abbot, TQ12 4PU, UK

10 9 8 7 6 5 4 3 2 1

F+W Media publishes high quality books on a wide range of subjects
For more great book ideas visit www.fwmedia.co.uk